Imperfect Victories

LAW IN THE AMERICAN WEST
Series Editor
John R. Wunder,
University of Nebraska–Lincoln
Volume 6

Mark R. Scherer

Imperfect Victories

*The Legal Tenacity
of the Omaha Tribe,
1945–1995*

University
of Nebraska Press
Lincoln & London

Portions of chapter 5, "The Legal Struggle for Blackbird
Bend, 1966–1995," were originally published in "Imperfect
Victory: The Legal Struggle for Blackbird Bend" by Mark R.
Scherer, *Annals of Iowa*, Vol. 57 (Winter 1998), pp. 38–71.
Copyright 1998 State Historical Society of Iowa. Reprinted
by permission of the publisher.

♾

Library of Congress Cataloging-in-Publication Data
Scherer, Mark R.
    Imperfect victories : the legal tenacity of the Omaha
Tribe, 1945–1995 / Mark R. Scherer.
        p.   cm. — (Law in the American West ; v. 6)
    Includes bibliographical references and index.
    ISBN 0-8032-4251-4 (cloth : alk. paper)
    1. Omaha Indians—Government policy. 2. Omaha
Indians—Legal status, laws, etc. 3. Omaha Indians—Land
tenure. 4. United States—Trials, litigation, etc. 5. United
States—Race relations. I. Title. II. Series.
E99.O4S34   1999   98-37507
323.1'19752—dc21   CIP

Contents

List of Illustrations / vii

Acknowledgments / ix

Introduction / xi

1. The Arrival of Public Law 280 on the Omaha Reservation, 1946–1953 / 1

2. Public Law 280 in Operation and the Battle over Retrocession, 1953–1970 / 25

3. The Omaha Experience with Indian Claims Commission Case 225, 1951–1964 / 47

4. Round Two before the Indian Claims Commission—Case 138, 1951–1966 / 69

5. The Legal Struggle for Blackbird Bend, 1966–1995 / 89

Conclusion / 115

Notes / 119

Index / 161

Illustrations

TABLE

Prosecution of Indians, Thurston County, Nebraska,
1946–1948 / 22

MAPS

1. Thurston County, Nebraska / 41
2. Omaha Cession, 1854 / 55
3. Cession 151 territory / 73
4. Cession 151 territory, depicting Platte Purchase and Iowa
   Assignment areas / 76
5. Missouri River at Blackbird Bend / 94
6. Missouri River at Monona Bend and Omaha Mission Bend / 103

PHOTOGRAPHS

1. Omaha children enjoying new bicycles / 65
2. Omaha tribal members display copy of 1854 treaty / 95
3. Omaha tribal members outside cottage at Blackbird Bend / 98
4. CasinOmaha / 114
5. Omaha tribal farming operations at Blackbird Bend / 114

Acknowledgments

Although the inevitable errors of fact or interpretation in this book belong to me alone, a great number of other people deserve credit for whatever merit it may possess. Deep appreciation goes first to my mentor and friend, Dr. Michael Tate. His skills as a teacher, writer, and editor have set the academic standards that I seek to emulate. In addition, his bibliography on the Omaha Tribe of Nebraska is the definitive starting point for all research related to the Omahas. Many of the resources I used in this project would likely have gone untapped were it not for that invaluable guide. Dr. John Wunder has also been most indulgent with his time in guiding this project to completion, and he has become a much-appreciated editor and advisor as well. Marvin Bergman of the State Historical Society of Iowa fine-tuned an earlier version of chapter 5 for publication in *The Annals of Iowa*, and he has been most gracious in his comments and assistance. The result is a much better finished product. Special thanks also to Dr. Jerold Simmons, not only for his valuable insights on the legal and constitutional issues addressed herein, but also for his continuing encouragement and guidance on other projects as well.

The staff of the Federal Records Center in Kansas City, particularly archivists Michael Brodhead and Clara Rowland, were most cooperative during my work at their facility. Similarly, archivist Dennis Bilger of the Harry S. Truman Presidential Library went out of his way to help me retrieve valuable materials from the Dillon Myer and Phileo Nash papers on deposit there. Special thanks also to Martha Koch, Deputy Clerk in charge at the Federal District Court for the Northern District of Iowa in Sioux City, who was extremely generous with both her time and her files in helping me piece together the story of the

Blackbird Bend litigation. Back here at home, cartographer Marvin Barton of the University of Nebraska–Omaha patiently drafted and redrafted the maps found herein, with consistent good humor and wonderful results.

Omaha tribal members Doran Morris Sr., Wynema Morris, and Ed Zendejas, among others, indulged my requests for interviews and offered important personal perspectives on past and current issues confronting the tribe. Thanks also to Judy Boughter, who forged the path for this study with her remarkable synthesis of the Omahas' history during the eighteenth and nineteenth centuries and kindly shared many of her research materials with me.

My deepest and most personal thanks go to my family. My parents and in-laws have given me unflagging encouragement throughout this project. My sons Ben, Eric, and Philip have always been available to remind me of the things that are most important in life and to divert me with the sports and other activities we enjoy. Finally, and most importantly, I am indebted to my wife and best friend, Lisa, for her patience and understanding during what must be the most prolonged career transition in recorded history. Her skills as a teacher and scholar have been the inspiration for my work, and her love and support have quite literally made this effort possible.

Introduction

The notion that federal Indian policy has vacillated wildly over this nation's 220 years of existence has become a tired but true cliché. Countless scholars, legislative committees, and ad hoc task forces have chronicled the pendulum swing of Indian relations between the disparate goals of forced assimilation, on the one hand, and tribal self-determination, on the other. Not quite as commonplace, however, are examinations of the specific ways in which the historical ebb and flow of broad government policy has affected individual tribes and reservations. More studies of this latter sort are needed because only at the grassroots level can the tangible, human effects of the shifting tides of federal policy be truly assessed.

This book seeks to examine the localized effects of recent federal policymaking in the context of one Native American nation—the Omaha Tribe of Nebraska. Over the past five decades, this remarkably resilient tribe has fought back within the system against government actions some of which date back more than 150 years. The Omahas have become notably tenacious legal warriors, achieving a prominence in the annals of federal Indian relations that belies their relatively small population and their relatively obscure geographic presence in northeastern Nebraska. Although the Omahas are far from prosperous today, they have achieved a cultural and economic renaissance in the 1980s and 1990s that can be traced in large part to their legal perseverance over the last fifty years. Ultimately, then, what follow are the stories of "imperfect victories"—legislative and judicial struggles that resulted, sometimes in failure, but more often in at least partial success for the Omahas. And in the "imperfections" of these legal victories may be discerned many of the lingering problems in the realm of Indian relations today.

While the focus here is on contemporary issues, the common wisdom of historical analysis cautions that context is everything. It is, therefore, useful to indulge in a brief overview of the history of the Omahas, in order to establish an appropriate context for what follows.[1] The people who would ultimately be called the Omaha Tribe of Nebraska came to the Great Plains several hundred years ago, migrating west with their close relatives the Poncas from a "wooded country near a great body of water."[2] By 1775, the Omahas had separated from the Ponca and had established a home territory in what is today northeastern Nebraska, centered on their "Large Village" along Omaha Creek.[3] The eighteenth-century Omahas practiced a seminomadic Plains Indian lifestyle, spending about three months of each year in their earth-lodge villages cultivating corn, beans, pumpkins, and squash, and ranging far out onto the plains on both sides of the Missouri River for their semiannual bison hunts—generally held in the early summer after planting and again in the late fall after the harvest.[4]

The Omahas' spiritual life centered on Umon'hon'ti, the Sacred Pole, also known as the Venerable Man. According to tribal history, the Pole had been "a gift from Wakon'da," the Great Spirit, cut from a luminous burning tree whose fire could be seen only at night. Umon'hon'ti served as a deeply powerful symbol of tribal identity, unity, and authority and was preserved through the years by a succession of honored priests or "Keepers."[5] As tribal fortunes declined through the nineteenth century, the Sacred Pole ultimately found its way to the Peabody Museum at Harvard University, where it was housed as an obscure ethnocultural relic until 1989, when it was returned to the tribe after a long and emotional campaign by the Omahas and their supporters. The story of the Sacred Pole and its return to the Omahas has been the subject of great academic and popular attention, including a recently published book by anthropologist Robin Ridington and Omaha tribal historian Dennis Hastings.[6]

Although it is difficult to pinpoint exactly when whites first made contact with the Omahas, the tribe was known to French fur traders as early as 1724. Through the 1700s, the tribe generally prospered, becoming increasingly enmeshed in the burgeoning and lucrative European fur trade along the middle Missouri. The two decades from about 1780 to 1800 were the glory years for the Omahas. Under the leadership of their enigmatic and controversial chief, Black Bird, the well-armed Omahas were able to force traders coming upriver to stop, unload their wares, and bargain for safe passage. So powerful was Black Bird's presence that French, Spanish, and English traders could not hope to succeed without gaining and keeping the great chief's favor. When Spanish trader James Mackay constructed a cabin and trading post near the Omaha's Large Village in 1795, he advised his company that Black Bird was "more despotic than any European prince" and instructed them to ensure that the chief receive a suitably prestigious gift every year.[7]

The Omahas' golden age did not last long. Like so many of their native brethren across the country, they were brought down, not by the Europeans' guns, but by their germs. A smallpox epidemic swept through the tribe in the winter of 1800–1801, killing Chief Black Bird, and reducing the tribe's population by as much as one-half.[8] Their longtime enemies the Sioux quickly took advantage of the Omahas' weakened condition and unsettled leadership, sweeping down from the north in the years immediately after the epidemic to ravage the tribe in murderous raids. By 1810, the once-powerful Omahas had lost control of their northeastern Nebraska territory to the Sioux. Reduced to near starvation and nomadic wandering, the tribe attempted to regroup farther to the south along the Elkhorn River, but Sioux attacks continued. By 1815, the Omahas were thought by some whites to be teetering on the brink of extinction.[9]

It was at this low ebb of Omaha existence that the tribe first entered into a formalized relationship with the young American government. On July 20, 1815, several Omaha chiefs and warriors executed a "treaty of peace and friendship" by which the tribe purported to place itself under the exclusive protection of the United States. This ostensibly innocuous Portage des Sioux Treaty of 1815 would prove to have far-reaching consequences for the tribe—a fateful first step in what would become a long series of ill-fated treaties with the U.S. government. Those treaties, some of which are detailed in later chapters, resulted in massive land cessions that culminated in the tribe's seminal 1854 treaty, wherein it relinquished all its traditional homelands in return for a 300,000-acre reservation in the Black Bird Hills of northeastern Nebraska.

Omaha fortunes continued to decline after the tribe's confinement to the new reservation. Depredations by the Sioux continued, despite assurances to the Omahas that they would be protected by the United States. White settlers and land speculators, unsatisfied with Indian control of the fertile and picturesque Black Bird Hills area, crowded the reservation from all sides. Promised annuities of consumer goods were chronically late in arriving and often of inferior quality. As whites pushed farther onto the plains, the bison became increasingly scarce, until eventually that "pillar of the Omahas' traditional life" was eliminated.[10] Through it all, however, the Omahas' fields continued to produce excellent yields, and their population actually increased slightly during the 1860s to a total of 1,020 by 1870.[11]

Ironically, it was the Omahas' perceived success on the reservation during the 1860s and 1870s that would lead to further government attempts to undermine their tribal identity through assimilationist "reforms." Beginning in the 1870s, and continuing virtually to this day, the Omahas have borne more than their fair share of the burden of shifting government policies. Indeed, since the establishment of the reservation in northeastern Nebraska in 1854, the Omahas have served involuntarily as sociological guinea pigs in the laboratory of federal Indian policy, with each new program contributing, until recently, to a cumulatively disastrous effect on the tribe's culture and economy.

The Omahas suffered particularly grievous consequences as a result of the assimilationist initiatives pushed through Congress in the late 1800s by various eastern reform groups that came to be known collectively as the "Friends of the Indian." The centerpiece of the reformers' program was a move toward detribalization through the allotment of reservation lands to individual Indians. In 1882, the Omahas became one of the first tribes in the nation to undergo the allotment process, pursuant to a statute enacted largely at the behest of the tribe's most renowned white "benefactor," Alice Fletcher. Fletcher's role in the story of the Omahas' ultimate dispossession cannot be overstated. She unquestionably possessed a sincere and deeply felt interest in the tribe's well-being and no doubt believed that her actions would help the Omahas survive and thrive. Indeed, her vigorous campaign for allotment on the Omaha reservation was supported by many influential tribal members who, like her, believed that individual ownership of their land would protect them from removal to Indian Territory and provide a legacy for their children.[12]

Despite those good intentions, allotment proved disastrous to the tribe on every front—economic, social, and cultural. Racked by pervasive poverty, alcoholism, and other social ills, many Omahas leased their allotments to white farmers or speculators. Even more sold their lands outright. By 1910, 50,000 acres of Omaha land had been lost, and, forty-five years later, the total had risen to more than 107,000 acres, leaving only about 28,000 acres of the tribe's formerly vast homelands in Omaha hands.[13]

Before the pernicious effect of the 1882 allotment procedures on tribal landholdings became fully known, government bureaucrats and assimilation advocates touted the Omaha experiment as a success, paving the way for the landmark 1887 Dawes Severalty Act, which extended the allotment program nationwide. As historian Michael Tate has observed, the net effect of the allotment programs first instituted on the Omaha reservation was "the impoverishment of Indians everywhere, the loss of more than ninety million acres of land once guaranteed by treaty, and the total assault upon Indian culture in the name of pragmatic assimilation."[14]

The twentieth century has seen a continuation of the Omahas' role as a sacrificial pawn in the chess game of Indian policymaking. As Indian Commissioner John Collier's relatively enlightened "Indian New Deal" of the 1930s gave way to the misguided postwar swing toward "termination," the Omaha reservation once again became the proving ground for a new direction in Indian policy. With the passage of Public Law (PL) 280 in 1953, the federal government transferred civil and criminal jurisdiction over the reservations in five selected states, including Nebraska, to state and local governments. As developments on the Omaha reservation would subsequently prove, virtually no one at the federal, state, or local level accurately envisioned the effect of that action on the designated reservations. Indeed, many Nebraska state officials proved to be woefully ignorant of the meaning and effect of PL 280 even years after its passage, despite the state's ostensible prior consent to its provisions.

Like the allotment experiments seventy years earlier, the transfer of federal criminal jurisdiction over the Omaha reservation to the state of Nebraska produced disastrous results. A combination of inadequate state funding and racial tension between the Omahas and their white neighbors in Thurston County brought lawlessness and jurisdictional chaos to the reservation. Thus, the Omahas again gained unwanted national prominence, this time as the unfortunate victims of the bureaucratic folly inherent in PL 280.

In part on the basis of the jurisdictional debacle on the Omaha reservation, in 1968 Congress amended PL 280 to allow states to retrocede Indian jurisdiction back to the federal government. Seeing an opportunity to rid itself of an expensive bureaucratic headache, but again not clearly understanding what it was doing, the state of Nebraska initially offered to return jurisdiction to the federal government. Its offer was accepted. Although the state later changed its mind and attempted to rescind its offer of retrocession, the federal courts negated that effort. The Omahas then became the first Indian tribe in the PL 280 states to escape state criminal jurisdiction. With retrocession, the tribe created its own police force and tribal court system, but conflicts between the Omahas and local law enforcement authorities concerning jurisdictional uncertainties continue to plague the county to this day.

The postwar years also saw a shift in federal policy regarding the resolution of Indian legal grievances stemming from two hundred years of broken treaties. With the creation of the Indian Claims Commission (ICC) in 1946, Congress sought to provide a "nonjudicial" forum for the final resolution of all lingering claims, as a precursor to the eventual termination of tribal existence and the full assimilation of Indians into white society. Like virtually every other tribe in the country, the Omahas took advantage of this new avenue of redress, filing two separate claims before the commission.

Just as the Omahas' experience with PL 280 and retrocession offers an instructive case study for the localized effect of those policies, so too does the tribe's experience before the ICC offer insight into the merits and the flaws of the commission's operations. While the Omahas ultimately prevailed in the prosecution of both their ICC claims, those successes came only after nearly twenty years of tedious and complex litigation. The Omahas also achieved another nationally significant first, as their pathbreaking compromise with the government forged the commission's "Omaha Rule" for the processing of similar settlements in dozens of other cases.

The resolution of the Omahas' ICC claims also demonstrates the unfortunate built-in limitations of the commission's remedial powers. As was the case in all judgments rendered by the ICC, the Omahas were not awarded interest on the amounts they finally received, thus leaving them substantially less than fully compensated for the injustices they had suffered. In addition, the receipt of the ICC judgment funds resulted in the development of disturbing intratribal factionalism over the distribution of proceeds. Controversies centering on the use of tribal funds occasionally plague the Omahas to this day, generally pitting tribal members who live in urban areas against those who live on the reservation.

In the 1970s and 1980s, the Omahas retained their prominence as legal warriors, waging a prolonged and incredibly complex judicial battle in which they sought to regain possession of more than eleven thousand acres situated east of the Missouri River. The tribe claimed that, before changes in the river channel, the land had been a part of its reservation; after the river channel moved west, however, the land was considered part of Iowa and was occupied over time by white farmers. The story of the Blackbird Bend litigation exposes several recurring and important aspects of modern Indian relations. Among those themes are issues relating to Indian political and legal activism, racial tensions between tribes and their white neighbors, and the often-controversial role of the federal government as the continuing trustee of Indian lands. The Blackbird Bend litigation is particularly noteworthy on the latter issue since the Omahas spent nearly as much energy fighting against U.S. representation of the tribe as they did in battling the white claimants in Iowa. As described in chapter 5 below, the Omahas ultimately gained an "imperfect victory" at Blackbird Bend, regaining a small portion of the land they sought, which has become the site of their currently profitable tribal gaming operation, CasinOmaha.

This book seeks to describe and interpret each of these episodes in the modern legal history of the Omaha tribe. The goal is not only to fill a void in the historical record by providing a synthesis of the facts but also to suggest ways in which the Omahas' experiences reflect the effect of larger trends in federal Indian policy over the past five decades. By their determined efforts to obtain that which they considered rightfully theirs, the Omahas provide a compelling example of a tribe struggling to preserve its unique cultural legacy in the face of daunting bureaucratic and judicial inertia. Theirs is a story that deserves to be told, one that will, one hopes, spur additional research directed toward the grassroots effect of federal Indian policy on both Native Americans and their non-Indian neighbors and countrymen.

Imperfect Victories

1. The Arrival of Public Law 280
on the Omaha Reservation,
1946–1953

A dragon's nest of legal and administrative confusion.
John Collier (1953)

On August 1, 1953, the U.S. House of Representatives adopted House Concurrent Resolution 108, announcing "the sense of the Congress" that certain Indian tribes should be "freed from federal supervision and control" as rapidly as possible.[1] Issued jointly with the Senate, the resolution explicitly proclaimed what had become implicitly apparent over the preceding few years—a congressional desire wholly to liquidate Indian tribalism and extinguish forever the government's unique trust relationship with Native Americans. Resolution 108 thus served as the federal government's first overt step in furtherance of its ill-fated termination policy of the 1950s and 1960s.[2]

To this day, references to the termination era are disturbing to many Native Americans. The termination movement sought the most aggressively assimilationist result possible—the outright extinguishment of Indian tribes and the abrogation of all legal and trust relationships between the federal government and the nation's Indians. While only a small percentage of Indian tribes would ultimately be "terminated," other congressional initiatives adopted in pursuit of the termination goal produced far more harm than benefit to Indian society. That was particularly the case on and around the Omaha reservation in Thurston County, Nebraska, where the terminationist measure that became known as PL 280 would have a devastating effect on the Omahas and all the other residents of the county. The PL 280 story cannot be fully understood, however, without an appreciation of the

1

origins and evolution of the terminationist sentiment on which it was based. Thus, a brief contextual review of developments in Indian policy during the first half of the twentieth century must be undertaken.

The assimilationist movement of the 1880s and 1890s (briefly described in the introduction) continued with a vengeance into the 1900s. As allotment of tribal lands continued, the Indian land base was relentlessly eroded, and Indians lost virtually all elements of sovereignty and control over their dwindling resources. By 1920, the secretary of the interior had acquired extensive jurisdiction to compel the continuing acculturation of Indians through, among other powers, the unilateral authority to distribute tribal funds held in trust, lease unallotted tribal lands, and control Indians' testamentary disposition of property.[3]

Just as the all-out assault on "Indianness" reached its zenith in the mid-1920s, an opposing viewpoint began to emerge. The primary catalyst for a new direction in Indian policy was the publication in 1928 of the "Meriam Report" on Indian conditions in the United States.[4] A full examination of this renowned and influential study is beyond my scope here.[5] Suffice it to say, however, that the Meriam Report revealed shamefully inadequate health care, sanitation, and educational facilities, corrupt and confusing legal systems, and pervasive poverty and cultural despair throughout Indian society. From a policy standpoint, the most significant conclusions contained in the report were that the allotment system and the program of forced acculturation pursued over the preceding forty years had been a dismal failure and were the major causes of Native Americans' deplorable condition.

The Meriam Report set the stage for a new direction in federal Indian policy, a period that would come to be known as the "Collier era." As Franklin Roosevelt's New Deal transformed American society, his commissioner of Indian affairs, John Collier, moved aggressively to bring similarly wide-ranging changes to the arena of federal Indian policy. During his tenure from 1933 to 1945, Collier played a key role in forging an "Indian New Deal," based in large part on the passage and implementation of the landmark Indian Reorganization Act (IRA) of 1934. The enactment of the IRA gave Collier the enabling legislation he needed to effectuate the cornerstones of his Indian New Deal—the cessation of the allotment process and the implementation of a new system of Indian sovereignty and self-government.

Under the IRA, tribes were authorized to establish new mechanisms of self-government pursuant to newly drafted tribal constitutions. If and when such constitutions were adopted, the tribes could charter tax-exempt corporations to control tribal funds, manage unallotted tribal property, and create businesses designed to promote economic development on the reservations. Elections were to be held on all reservations to determine whether a particular tribe wished to come under the provisions of the IRA. Legislative maneuvering initially exempted some groups, most notably the numerous tribes in Oklahoma and Alaska, from the provisions of the act. Ultimately, only 37 percent of the tribes eligible to approve the IRA and adopt constitutions opted to do so voluntarily.[6] In subsequent years, the Department of the Interior and Collier's own Bureau of Indian Affairs (BIA) exerted institutional and administrative pressures on the "unorganized" tribes, ultimately forcing many of them to succumb to IRA procedures.

Generalizations regarding John Collier's legacy are both difficult and dangerous. His initiatives were certainly not unanimously endorsed throughout Indian society. Many Indian groups viewed his New Deal, which was often unilaterally and autocratically imposed without widespread Indian consent, as resonating with a paternalism that was similar to, if not as virulent as, that of the assimilationists. Others observed that the new sovereignty that was ostensibly granted to them under the IRA was really nothing more, and perhaps considerably less, than the sovereignty they had always possessed and asserted.[7]

Those misgivings notwithstanding, it is fair to conclude that Collier's New Deal did, as the label suggests, mark a new beginning for Indian tribes. Even before the passage of the IRA, Collier used his administrative authority to stop the assimilationist assault on Indian culture and religion and took steps designed to "restore a sense of Indian community."[8] By the 1940s, the IRA and Collier's related executive actions had brought marginally improved conditions to many Native Americans. The landgrab was largely, if temporarily, stopped, and new tribal governments were taking tentative steps in furtherance of their reconfirmed sovereignty and cultural rebirth. Whatever cautious optimism may have emerged among the tribes would prove to be short-lived, however, as the specter of termination loomed on the horizon.

Assimilationist sentiment had not, of course, simply evaporated during the Collier era. Indeed, congressional opposition to the IRA and Collier's other initiatives was widespread throughout his tenure. With Collier's resignation in 1945, various legislative proposals emerged calling for the repeal or rollback of the IRA. Those efforts were based in part on yet another special task force investigation of the country's continuing "Indian problem." Standing in stark contrast to the conclusions reached in the Meriam Report a generation earlier, the 1949 Hoover Commission Report prescribed the "complete integration" of Native Americans into mainstream society, via the eventual elimination of all BIA services.[9] Thus did the pendulum of Indian policy once again swing back toward assimilation, a shift in direction that would culminate in Resolution 108 and the ensuing terminationist legislation.[10]

Even before Congress was able to act on the Hoover Commission's recommendations, however, a new commissioner of Indian affairs had moved forward aggressively to reverse the Collier-era initiatives and implement a terminationist ideology. Dillon S. Myer, who served as commissioner of Indian affairs in the Truman administration from May 1950 to March 1953 and had previously overseen the internment of Japanese Americans as director of the War Relocation Authority during World War II, wasted no opportunity to advance an agenda of decentralization and eventual withdrawal of BIA services from Indian tribes.[11] In a letter to all tribal council members dated October 10, 1952, Myer clearly delineated the bureau's aims:

> The policy of the Bureau of Indian Affairs with respect to withdrawal contemplates two major objectives: (1) that the responsibility which the Bureau now has for providing Indians with such services as education, health, welfare assistance, and law enforcement should be transferred to the agencies of State or local government which normally provide such services for other citizens, and (2) that the responsibility for supervision of Indian trust property should be transferred to the Indians themselves—either as individuals or as tribal groups."[12]

4

Myer pursued those objectives aggressively, frequently sounding the need to move further and faster in the direction of termination.[13]

The congressional proponents of termination, including most notably Senator Hugh Butler of Nebraska, needed little convincing. Butler was among the most vocal of a growing bloc of western congressmen who sought once again to move Native Americans involuntarily into the mainstream of society. The terminationists aspired to "free" Indians, not by way of privatization of tribal lands, as had been the case in the earlier allotment era, but rather by the outright extinguishment of tribal existence. As early as 1947, Butler introduced legislation in the Senate aimed at "emancipating Indians from Federal wardship and control" by eliminating the BIA.[14] In 1950, he argued that the "paternalistic trappings" of federal wardship were "increasingly distasteful" to Indians and asked rhetorically, "Does the Indian desire to be considered Uncle Sam's stepchild forever?"[15] Again in 1951, he warned, "The Indian Bureau will not go voluntarily. It has been nourished and warmed too long. It will have to be kicked out by the Congress."[16]

Among the other proponents of termination, Senator Arthur Watkins of Utah, sometimes referred to as the "godfather of termination," couched his arguments for the "emancipation" of Indians in terms that today appear at best ridiculously overwrought and at worst blatantly disingenuous. Writing in support of the terminationist ideology, Watkins gushed: "Following in the footsteps of the Emancipation Proclamation of ninety-four years ago, I see the following words emblazoned in letters of fire above the heads of the Indians—THESE PEOPLE SHALL BE FREE!"[17] With similarly misguided fervor, Representative William H. Harrison of Wyoming, one of the sponsors of Resolution 108, succinctly noted its purpose by stating that it was designed to "free" the Indians from federal supervision and was "intended as a directive to the Bureau of Indian Affairs to start working itself out of a job."[18]

The new direction in policy did not go unchallenged. The National Congress of American Indians urged its members to resist the impending termination programs and bitterly criticized Dillon Myer for his "stated intention of working, to the subordination of all else, for the

5

abandonment of the Federal Government's trusteeship responsibilities guaranteed to many of you in your treaties."[19] The National Farmer's Union voiced its opposition as well, issuing a resolution in which it vowed to "continue to oppose the revocation of treaties and abandonment of the Indian to rapacious, selfish groups who want the resources on the Indian lands."[20] Other observers expressed their opposition in similar terms, viewing the shift in policy as "a sweeping betrayal of trust," and seeing the purported "liberation" of the Indians as nothing more than a smoke screen for a renewed landgrab by non-Indians.[21]

Not surprisingly, John Collier was one of the most vocal critics of the termination ideology, calling it a "compulsive torrent" that had been "stampeded through Congress," ushering in a new "century of dishonor."[22] Collier aimed some of his sharpest rhetoric directly at Dillon Myer, describing his tenure as "a coercive, stereotyped and dictatorial one-track drive toward the destruction of Indian rights and specifically toward the throwing of all Indian properties 'to the wolves.'"[23]

Notwithstanding that contemporary criticism, some modern commentators are relatively charitable in their evaluation of Congress's intent, suggesting that the terminationist ideology may have been based on true idealism, legitimate budgetary concerns, or the "anticolonialist spirit of the post–WW II period."[24] Myer himself was certainly a true believer to the end, regardless of Indian sentiment. In a memorandum to the secretary of the interior issued on the day he left office, he frankly acknowledged that the great majority of Indians seemed opposed to his withdrawal programs. Still, he maintained that "trusteeship and other special forms of government services to the Indians are holding the Indians back politically, socially and economically" and urged that "a strong hand be taken by both this Department and the Congress" to implement the withdrawal programs.[25]

Regardless of whether the political dynamics and motivations of the termination movement are viewed as benevolent or exploitative in nature, the results of termination proved to be disastrous for those tribes that actually experienced the process. For example, the Omahas' neighbors and historic relatives, the Northern Ponca, were terminated in 1962 and suffered grievous social and economic deprivation for some twenty years before being restored to tribal status in

1990.[26] The two most extensive and notorious terminations were those of the Klamaths of Oregon and the Menominees of Wisconsin in 1954. Both tribes' lands were quickly dissipated, and they were plunged into even deeper economic distress than they had previously suffered.[27] In all, 109 tribes were terminated during the 1950s and 1960s, resulting in countless tragic consequences, including the liquidation of more than 1.3 million acres of tribal land.[28]

While the Omahas were never actually terminated, the federal government's new direction in Indian policy would nevertheless affect the tribe in quite tangible ways. There is no clear evidence, either in the written record or in the memories of tribal members who have discussed the issue, regarding the tribe's viewpoint *before* the termination legislation began to be implemented. Indeed, as we shall see, the question of the Omahas' purported prior consent to a key piece of terminationist legislation that *did* directly affect them remains an enigma to this day. It is apparent, however, that, as the disastrous effect of termination on other tribes became evident, Omaha opposition to termination emerged and evolved along the same lines as that of most other interested observers. Thus begins the story of PL 280 on the Omaha reservation—a story that reflects the grassroots effect of ill-advised federal policy on both Native Americans and non-Indians who live on or around their reservations.

Just two weeks after the adoption of Resolution 108, Congress took the first substantive step in furtherance of its newly announced "sense" that Indian tribes ought to be terminated. Pressured by the termination bloc in Congress (including Nebraska Senator Hugh Butler, who sent a personal telegram to the White House), President Dwight Eisenhower signed into law Public Law 83-280 (PL 280) on September 15, 1953.[29] The new statute provided that the state of Nebraska and four other "mandatory" states were to assume both civil and criminal jurisdiction over all "Indian country" within their boundaries.[30] Other states were authorized to pass legislation or amend their constitutions so as to assume such jurisdiction at their option.[31] The jurisdictional chaos that would result from this misguided legislation, coupled with other adverse effects of the termination push, would eventually lead to the renouncement of the entire policy and the close of the termination era some fifteen years later. In the meantime, however, the law enforcement and jurisdictional problems arising on the Omaha reservation in northeast Nebraska made it the textbook example of the legislative folly inherent in the PL 280 scheme.

The legislative history of PL 280 indicates that its sponsors were ostensibly motivated by concern over the confusing and overlapping jurisdictional bounds between state, federal, and tribal law enforcement services and the resulting problems of law enforcement on and around specific reservations.[32] The Senate Report of the bill provides: "As a practical matter, the enforcement of law and order among the Indians . . . has been left largely to the Indian groups themselves. In many states, tribes are not adequately organized to perform that function; consequently there has been created a hiatus in law enforcement authority that could best be remedied by conferring criminal jurisdiction on States indicating an ability and willingness to accept such responsibility."[33]

Various other reports and correspondence in the congressional records reflect extensive concern over the "intolerable situation of lawlessness" in and around certain reservations as a result of confusion over jurisdictional bounds. During 1952 hearings on several bills that would eventually be melded into PL 280, the House Subcommittee on Indian Affairs heard testimony describing Indian reservations as "legal no-man's lands" and decrying the "complete breakdown of law and order on many of the reservations."[34] Significantly, there is no specific testimony or evidence in the legislative history regarding the law enforcement situation on the Omaha reservation in 1953, even from Nebraska Senator Hugh Butler, who was heavily involved with the hearings and debate. While conditions there were in fact quite poor, the passage of PL 280 would exacerbate the problem rather than alleviate it.

Much of the criticism of the PL 280 scheme, both before and after the bill's passage, focused on the absence of any provision requiring the consent of the affected Indian tribes to the transfer of jurisdiction. Eisenhower himself expressed "grave doubts" about this "unfortunate" omission from the bill. He signed it nevertheless, having apparently been advised that all Indians in the five mandatory states had been consulted and "enthusiastically endorsed" the legislation, and believing that "its basic purpose represents still another step in granting equality to all Indians in our nation." He went on to urge Congress to amend the bill in the upcoming session so as to require consultation with the tribes prior to the enactment of legislation subjecting them to state control.[35]

Notwithstanding Eisenhower's indulgent attitude toward the act's basic intent, John Collier and many other critics were less sanguine about both the law's purpose and its likely effect. The *New York Times* editorialized against the bill, stating that it had been "whipped through Congress so rapidly that practically no one interested in Indian affairs—least of all the Indians themselves—knew what was happening until it had already happened" and that "it could do great wrong to the American Indian population of many states." The paper went on to note that many of the interest groups that opposed the bill, including the Association on American Indian Affairs, the Institute of Ethnic Affairs, and the American Civil Liberties Union, were "only now beginning to be heard."[36] Collier was particularly prophetic in his criticism of the bill, accurately predicting that it would lead to "a dragon's nest of legal and administrative confusion."[37] He expressed dismay and bewilderment at the fact that Eisenhower had signed the bill despite his recognition of its "most un-Christian" approach.[38]

As to the Indians in the five mandatory states, the proponents of PL 280 were artfully vague in their handling of the consent issue. In a letter to the House Committee on Interior and Insular Affairs dated July 7, 1953, Assistant Secretary of the Interior Orme Lewis indicated that the Bureau of Indian Affairs had consulted with state and local authorities, as well as with Indian groups in the five mandatory states of California, Minnesota, Nebraska, Oregon, and Wisconsin, and had reported that all the states had "indicated their willingness to accept the proposed transfer of jurisdiction." The Indian groups in those states were likewise reported to be, "for the most part, agreeable to the transfer."[39]

Lewis acknowledged that several tribes had objected to the proposed transfer, contending that they would be subjected to inequitable treatment in the state courts and that their tribal police organizations were already capable of maintaining order on the reservations. Congress ultimately concluded that the tribal law enforcement operations on the Red Lake reservation in Minnesota, the Warm Springs reservation in Oregon, and the Menominee reservation in Wisconsin were indeed functioning in a satisfactory manner, and it specifically exempted them from the provisions of the bill.[40]

Lewis's representation to Congress that the Indians in Nebraska had been, "for the most part, agreeable" to the transfer of jurisdiction to the state had been preceded by similar congressional testimony from Commissioner Dillon Myer. Notwithstanding his ardent terminationist philosophy, Myer did urge Congress to consult with the affected tribes before the proposed transfer of jurisdiction because of the "varying situation" in each of the states with respect to law enforcement concerns. At a February 28, 1952, hearing before the Subcommittee on Indian Affairs, Myer proffered the *only* direct reference to the Nebraska situation in the entire legislative history of the bill. Explaining why no Nebraska tribes would be exempted from coverage, Myer stated, "Nebraska, I believe, would cover the whole State, *because we have gotten in touch with the tribes there*" (emphasis added).[41] Six months later, Myer made substantially the same representation at a meeting with his agency superintendents held at Aberdeen, South Dakota. There, Myer indicated that the bureau had consulted with the individual tribes in each of the mandatory states and that no tribe that objected to the transfer was included in the bill's coverage.[42]

Four years after PL 280 went into effect, Winnebago Agency superintendent Allen M. Adams presented a slightly more specific assertion of the supposed prior acquiescence of the Nebraska tribes. In a report delivered to the conference "Indian Problems of Law and Order" at the University of South Dakota in June 1957, Adams stated: "You've heard the remarks here that the Indians in Nebraska are now under Public Law 280. Before those Indians down there came under that law, *the three active councils were contacted. All of them expressed their willingness to come under that law.* The board of supervisors of the two counties where the Indians are located, Thurston County and Knox County, also agreed to that. It was taken up with the Attorney General who also agreed to it" (emphasis added).[43]

10

BIA and Omaha tribal records appear to confirm these representations of Adams, Myer, and Lewis regarding the prior consent of the Omahas. On March 9, 1951, Adams's predecessor as superintendent of the Winnebago Agency, H. E. Bruce, convened a meeting of delegates from the four tribal councils under his jurisdiction (Omaha, Winnebago, Santee Sioux, and Ponca) for the purpose of discussing a matter that he described as "the proposed bill to confer civil and criminal jurisdiction over Indians on the State of Nebraska."[44] That meeting resulted in the adoption of a joint resolution in which the tribal delegates announced that they had "read, discussed, and carefully considered the draft of a proposed bill to confer on the State of Nebraska civil and criminal jurisdiction over Indians in the State" and that "sections 2 and 4 of said proposed bill meet with the approval of the Indians of said tribes and have their endorsement."[45] The resolution was signed by tribal chairman Amos Lamson on behalf of the Omahas and was certified by Superintendent Bruce as having been adopted unanimously.

In the light of this apparent indication of consent by the tribe and the congressional testimony of Myer and Lewis on the issue, it is easy to understand President Eisenhower's belief that the Omahas and other Indians affected by the transfer of jurisdiction "enthusiastically endorsed" the passage of PL 280. Nevertheless, several factors in the historical record serve to cloud the issue of the Omahas' consent. In the first place, the March 9, 1951, resolution precedes the actual passage of PL 280 by more than two years. The resolution is not specific as to the precise piece of legislation being considered, nor does it specify the contents of "sections 2 and 4" of the bill, the only provisions endorsed by the tribe. The resolution thus does not definitively establish that the Omahas knowingly consented to the provisions of PL 280 as they ultimately emerged.

Moreover, the Omaha tribe was subject to the same factionalization and political infighting that characterize any other government entity. Given the two-year gap between the adoption of the 1951 resolution and the enactment of PL 280, it is entirely possible that the political sentiments of the tribe and its leadership may have changed in the interim. Alternatively, there is some reason to suspect that the actions of

11

the tribal representatives at the 1951 meeting may not have accurately reflected the attitude of the tribal membership as a whole.

Again, the records relating to H. E. Bruce's tenure as superintendent of the Winnebago Agency offer some insight into the latter possibility. In a May 16, 1949, report to the commissioner that is notable for both its thoroughness and its patronizing tone, Bruce provided his own subjective assessment of the character and abilities of each of the members of the Omaha Tribal Council. Writing of tribal chairman Amos Lamson (who would sign the 1951 "consent resolution" on behalf of the Omahas), Bruce stated, "[Lamson's] thinking is rather superficial. He is only one-quarter or less Indian, does not speak the Omaha language and will have difficulty maintaining a position of tribal leadership for these reasons." He went on to note that other tribal members "resent his present efforts to help the agency overcome [other problems described in the report]." Other council members were variously described as "unscrupulous and shiftless," "a slow and shallow thinker," or "motivated by a desire to feather his own nest."[46]

In a subsequent memorandum to the Aberdeen area director, Superintendent Bruce described Lamson as being "motivated first, last, and always by personal interest. . . . He is thoroughly insincere and unreliable."[47] Bruce recorded this assessment on March 1, 1951, just eight days *before* Lamson signed the "consent resolution" on behalf of the Omaha tribe. That resolution would be the only formal indication of the government's consultation with the Omahas regarding PL 280—a law that would in fact not even be enacted until more than two years after this questionable "endorsement" by the "unreliable" Lamson.

An even more tangible and troubling indication of the uncertainty surrounding the Omahas' consent to PL 280 may be found in a 1953 congressional investigatory report on the Bureau of Indian Affairs. In July 1952, Congress authorized the House Committee on Interior and Insular Affairs to conduct a comprehensive investigation of the BIA in order to recommend steps that would effectuate the withdrawal of all federal supervision and control over Indians as rapidly as possible.[48] To perform this investigation, a special subcommittee was created, which forwarded a request to the commissioner of Indian affairs for a report from the BIA addressing numerous specific issues related to the ultimate termination goal.

The commissioner, in turn, sent a memorandum to all bureau officials ordering that certain data be gathered from each reservation in order to facilitate the ultimate withdrawal of bureau services. One of the specific tasks assigned to agency officials was to ascertain the attitudes of Indians, state officials, and county officials with respect to the transfer of law-and-order jurisdiction over the reservation to the state. The responses to that inquiry were compiled and summarized in table XII attached to the final committee report, titled "Data on Reservation Law and Order." Contrary to the representations of Lewis, Myer, and Adams, and in sharp contrast to the apparent effect of the 1951 "consent resolution," the Omaha Indians in Nebraska are clearly indicated as being "*not favorable*" to the proposed transfer.[49]

Additional evidence that the Omahas were not necessarily willing participants in the PL 280 experiment may be found in the text of an appellate brief filed with the Nebraska Supreme Court in 1970. Arguing on behalf of an Omaha tribal member who had been convicted in state court of the murder of another Indian, the defendant's attorney, Lawrence E. Murphy, challenged the constitutional validity of PL 280's jurisdictional transfer. Murphy asserted that "no referendum of the members of the Omaha Indian Tribe" had been conducted prior to the transfer of jurisdiction to the state in 1953 and that therefore the purported abrogation of their rights under federal law was constitutionally infirm.[50]

While Murphy's 1970 statement was unsubstantiated, the question of the Omahas' consent is further obscured by the statements of tribal representative Alfred Gilpin at the same 1957 conference where Allen Adams had indicated the tribe's prior consent. Gilpin did not directly refute Adams's statement (he had been delayed by bad weather and was not present at the conference when Adams gave his report), but he repeatedly and bitterly lamented the "damage" and "destruction" caused by its passage.[51] Thus, whatever endorsement of the transfer of jurisdiction may have existed among the Omahas prior to 1953 had wholly evaporated within just a few years.

However intriguing the question of the Omahas' consent to PL 280 may be, it is equally significant to note that the precise nature of the state of Nebraska's apparent approval of the bill remains just as murky as that of the Omahas. In the light of PL 280's disastrous effects, a good deal of post hoc finger-pointing on that issue occurred among state officials. It appears that the only actual expression of the state's acquiescence took the form of a letter from state attorney general Clarence S. Beck dated July 26, 1951, to Winnebago Agency superintendent H. E. Bruce, in which Beck indicated that the then-pending bill for transfer of jurisdiction "seems to be in proper order and [that] this office has no objection to [its passage]."[52] While that letter predated the passage of PL 280 by more than two years, no further indication of the state's willingness to assume jurisdiction is apparent in the historical record.

Senator Hugh Butler's influence, combined with these dubious expressions of Indian and state consent, offers the only discernible explanation as to why Nebraska was among the mandatory PL 280 states. At a time when the BIA was searching the country for tribes that were willing to remove themselves from federal jurisdiction and states that appeared willing to accept the transfer of that jurisdiction, the expressions of acquiescence reflected in the Omahas' April 1951 "consent resolution" and Attorney General Beck's letter later that year offered the BIA the paper trail it needed to include Nebraska in PL 280's mandatory coverage. Given the purported expressions of consent by the state and the Indians and Butler's continuing fervent support for the bill, Nebraska became a mandatory state with virtually no questions asked.

It is also instructive to note that an examination of local and statewide newspapers during the period in which PL 280 was being considered and enacted reveals very little public awareness of the transfer of jurisdiction from the federal government to the state. Moreover, even those few state and local officials who were aware of the bill's provisions seemed to have little appreciation of its meaning or likely effect. In a brief article published just a week before the passage of PL 280, the *Lincoln Sunday Journal and Star* noted the uncertainty among state officials regarding the bill's effect. In a passage that would prove to be a considerable understatement, the paper suggested that "some legal matters will undoubtedly be affected in the new bills. Presumably this would mean more work for the peace officials in counties containing the reservations."[53] Just as the *New York Times* had suggested, the passage of PL 280 seems to have been a fait accompli long before any substantial portion of the Nebraska populace, Indian or white, realized what was happening.[54]

Perhaps the apparent lack of public and government attention to the passage of PL 280 in 1953 may be explained by the most intriguing conclusion to be drawn from an examination of this law as it affected the Omaha reservation. Surprisingly, PL 280 made very little change in the day-to-day jurisdictional status of the reservation because the state of Nebraska had been erroneously exercising criminal jurisdiction over the Omahas for some seventy years prior to 1953![55] Enactment of PL 280 was therefore most likely viewed by Nebraska state officials, as well as by the Omahas who purportedly endorsed its passage, as little more than a congressional confirmation of the status quo. An understanding of this situation requires an examination of several conflicting decisions of the Nebraska Supreme Court and the federal courts. Those decisions reflected, and it can be argued contributed to, the uncertainty and confusion that has characterized criminal jurisdiction on the Omaha reservation throughout its existence. Ironically, that jurisdictional turmoil was not addressed, or even appreciably acknowledged, by the state or federal courts in Nebraska until well *after* the passage of PL 280, which had been designed to eliminate those very concerns.

The Nebraska Supreme Court most directly addressed the pre-1953 jurisdictional status of the Omaha reservation in *Robinson v Sigler* (1971).[56] In that case, Omaha tribal member Enoch Robinson had been tried and convicted in the Nebraska state courts for the 1969 murder of another Indian on the Omaha reservation.[57] Robinson sought a writ of habeas corpus from the Nebraska Supreme Court, arguing that the state did not have jurisdiction to prosecute an Indian for the murder of another Indian within the limits of the reservation. The bulk of the parties' arguments in *Robinson* were devoted to issues unrelated to the pre-1953 jurisdictional status of the reservation. In the course of its decision, however, the *Robinson* court noted in *dicta* that the state of Nebraska had been exercising both civil and criminal jurisdiction over the Omaha Indians since at least 1882, over seventy years *before* PL 280 purportedly gave the state the right to do so.

The claimed basis for this pre-1953 state jurisdiction was set out in the brief filed on behalf of the state by Attorney General Clarence A. H. Meyer, much of which was accepted by the court and repeated verbatim in its opinion. The state argued that it had been vested with criminal jurisdiction over Indians long prior to 1953 on the basis of the 1882 allotment statute that authorized the secretary of the interior to convey Omaha tribal land to individual members of the tribe and retain certain portions in trust for the tribe as common property.[58] The statute went on to provide that, on completion of the allotments, every member of the tribe "shall have the benefit of and be subject to the laws, both civil and criminal, of the State of Nebraska."[59] On the basis of that language, the *Robinson* court held that the state courts of Nebraska had "either concurrent or residual criminal jurisdiction" over the Omahas prior to 1953.[60] PL 280 had merely "confirmed it and gave it to the state conclusively and exclusively."[61]

The state's position on this issue was reiterated several years later in testimony before a Senate subcommittee considering the amendment or repeal of PL 280. On March 4, 1976, Nebraska assistant attorney general Ralph H. Gillan appeared before the Senate Subcommittee on Indian Affairs to present the views of the Nebraska Department of Justice with respect to the proposed Indian Law Enforcement Improvement Act of 1975. In the course of his testimony, Gillan matter-of-factly acknowledged that PL 280 had not appreciably changed the jurisdictional facts of life on the Omaha reservation:

> The history of jurisdiction over Indian country in Nebraska prior to 1953 is somewhat confusing, and it may well be that State jurisdiction was mistakenly exercised. . . . in any event, *it is clear that for many years before 1953 the Nebraska courts did exercise civil and criminal jurisdiction over Indians on the reservation,* apparently concurrently with the Federal courts. The exercise of this jurisdiction was not challenged before 1953. . . . State jurisdiction had, in fact been exercised, rightly or

wrongly, before 1953. In 1953, under Public Law 280, Nebraska acquired exclusive civil and criminal jurisdiction over all Indian country in Nebraska. *It probably did not involve any great exchange, as a practical matter, from what had gone on before.*[62] (emphasis added)

Gillan's statement was sufficiently provocative to prompt additional inquiry into the matter by the subcommittee. Senator James Abourezk asked the BIA to investigate and analyze the question of Nebraska's pre-1953 exercise of jurisdiction. The request resulted in a responsive memorandum dated March 24, 1976, from the Winnebago Agency superintendent to the director of the Aberdeen Area Office. The superintendent reported that, although he had been unable to locate agency records pertaining to law enforcement activities prior to 1953, through discussions with local residents he had determined that the state of Nebraska, specifically Thurston County, had indeed exercised both criminal and civil jurisdiction over Indians prior to the enactment of PL 280. The memorandum specifically recited conversations with various individuals, including Omaha tribal chairman Edward L. Cline and several persons connected with local law enforcement, in which each respondent confirmed that Indians were routinely arrested and prosecuted in the state courts of Nebraska prior to 1953.[63]

The Nebraska Supreme Court's decision in *Robinson v Sigler* thus served as both a confirmation of and an attempted justification for the de facto state of criminal jurisdiction on the Omaha reservation as it had existed for almost a century. Whatever clarity the state court may have thought it brought to this issue with *Robinson*, however, was quickly dissipated by the federal courts. In *Omaha Tribe v Village of Walthill* (1971), decided just five months after *Robinson*, the federal district court specifically rejected the state court's reliance on the 1882 allotment statute as the basis for its assertion of pre-1953 jurisdiction. The court held that the provisions of the allotment act had never been fully executed on the Omaha reservation and that therefore criminal jurisdiction within the reservation had not passed to the state of Nebraska by virtue of that statute.[64] Thus the "dragon's nest" remained intact.

While the state's exercise of jurisdiction prior to 1953 was almost certainly erroneous, the fact that it proceeded without challenge by the Omahas or the federal government for so many years offers a compelling illustration of the complex and confusing state of jurisdictional issues surrounding Indian reservations in the pre-1953 era. A complete examination of the historical background of jurisdiction in Indian territory is beyond my scope here.[65] Suffice it to say, however, that throughout American history the problem of criminal and civil jurisdiction over Indian lands has presented a chaotic and often conflicting morass of treaties, statutes, and regulations, resulting in what one commentator has accurately described as "a complex labyrinth which many practitioners and courts find virtually impossible to master."[66]

A great deal of this nationwide jurisdictional confusion stemmed, as it did in Nebraska, from the allotment ideology of the late 1800s and the piecemeal implementation of the various allotment statutes enacted during that era. Specifically, section 6 of the General Allotment Act of 1887 provided that Indians who were allotted lands under the act would thereafter be subject to the jurisdiction of the state courts, just as the 1882 act had been interpreted by the courts in Nebraska to confer jurisdiction on themselves, as the court held in *Robinson v Sigler*.

For several reasons, however, section 6 of the General Allotment Act did not have the anticipated effect of substantially shifting criminal jurisdiction over Indian lands to the states. In the first place, section 6 was never intended to create an exception to the exclusive jurisdiction of the federal courts over certain crimes committed on Indian reservations pursuant to the Federal Major Crimes Act. Furthermore, heirs of an allottee were deemed *not* subject to state jurisdiction, thus creating a totally unworkable practical dilemma for state law enforcement operations.[67] That operational dilemma was expressly recognized by the acting solicitor of the Department of the Interior when he wrote in a 1954 opinion letter to Assistant Secretary Orme Lewis:

> Such complexities and distinctions as these have rendered the grant of State jurisdiction over Indians contemplated by the general Allotment

18

Act largely ineffective. The sponsors of that legislation assumed that the allotment of the Indians in severalty would be but the prelude to the termination of their tribal relations. . . . When that program failed to be carried out, and the Indians . . . continued to maintain their tribal relations and the Government continued its guardianship over them, the subjection of the Indians to the jurisdiction of the States ceased to have much reality. State law enforcement officers could not, after all, go around with tract books in their pockets, and being unable to distinguish a patent-in-fee Indian from a ward Indian, they did not commonly concern themselves with law violations by Indians, and the theoretical jurisdiction of the States thus fell into innocuous desuetude.[68]

Given the jurisdictional complexities involved, the question of the state's culpability in erroneously exercising Indian jurisdiction prior to 1953 seems open to debate. On the one hand, counsel for Indian defendants in the pre–PL 280 years failed (perhaps understandably) to recognize and assert a lack-of-jurisdiction defense in state court proceedings that might well have freed their clients. Having assumed de facto if not de jure authority, state prosecutors and judges obviously took no steps to alert tribal leadership, Indian criminal defendants, or their counsel of the jurisdictional question, although it might be argued that they had that ethical obligation. Thus, the validity of countless criminal convictions of Indian defendants in the state courts prior to 1953 remains in question to this day. On the other hand, it would be unduly simplistic for modern observers to engage in sweeping criticism of the Nebraska courts for their invocation of jurisdiction over the Omahas. It can be plausibly argued that the state courts' exercise of jurisdiction prior to the passage of PL 280 was not so much a usurpation of power as it was an attempt to pick their way through a jurisdictional quagmire.

For example, in *Kitto v State* (1915), the Nebraska Supreme Court offered a compelling rationale for its exercise of jurisdiction in Indian cases. A Santee Sioux was charged in state court with misdemeanor assault arising out of a fight with another Santee on the Sioux reservation. The defendant filed a motion to dismiss in the trial court, arguing that his alleged crime "was an offense within the exclusive jurisdiction of the courts of the United States, and not within the jurisdiction of [the state] court." The trial court denied the defendant's motion, and the supreme court affirmed. Explaining its decision, the court noted that the only way to give meaning to the apparent intent of the nineteenth-century allotment statutes was to construe them so as to transfer jurisdiction to the state courts after the allotments were made. If such jurisdiction was not vested in the state, the court reasoned, it was vested nowhere. Indeed, this may have been the case on the Omaha reservation, where there was no viable tribal judiciary before the early 1970s. On other reservations, however, the tribes themselves were empowered to handle all nonmajor crimes. The *Kitto* court concluded that Congress could not have intended for nonmajor offenses to go completely unpunished and that therefore the Nebraska courts had no choice but to hear such cases, in order to provide "equal protection of the law . . . to all, both Indians and white men."[69]

Such rulings notwithstanding, by 1975 the state of Nebraska would itself expressly acknowledge that its pre-1953 criminal jurisdiction over Indian matters *should have been* limited to offenses committed by Indians *off* the reservation and offenses committed by non-Indians *on* the reservation.[70] The state's actual exercise of criminal jurisdiction over Indians in the years preceding PL 280, as reflected in *Kitto* and many other decisions, had far exceeded those bounds.[71] Still, whatever errors had occurred in the state's invocation of Indian jurisdiction prior to 1953 were in fact obviated by the enactment of PL 280. As a mandatory state, Nebraska gained absolute and exclusive jurisdiction at that time regardless of what had gone on before.[72]

Thus, the real effect of PL 280 on the Omaha reservation was not to alter the *entity* that exercised jurisdiction over Indian matters, for the state had been doing that for decades. What the new law changed was the pattern of criminal law *enforcement* operations on the Omaha reservation. An assessment of the effect of PL 280 on the reservation must therefore begin with a brief and admittedly cursory examination of the law enforcement situation in Thurston County in the years immediately preceding 1953.

While the precise statistics are difficult to track, there are ample indications that law-and-order conditions on and around the reservation were dismal before 1953.[73] Useful, albeit subjective, evidence of those conditions may be found in a May 16, 1949, report to the commissioner of Indian Affairs by Winnebago Agency superintendent H. E. Bruce. Bruce presented a bleak account of the abysmal social, economic, and law enforcement conditions on the Omaha reservation. In keeping with the assimilationist tenor of the times, Bruce scathingly criticized the attempts of the Collier-era administrators to foster tribal self-government and cultural revival among the Omahas:

> Since acceptance of the Indian Reorganization Act by the four Nebraska tribes . . . social problems which were vital and basic . . . have been neglected and ignored until they have become ugly sores. . . . Vicious social practices, once reasonably controlled, have multiplied with apparent official sanction and encouragement. . . . All this has served to intensify maladjustment, confusion, discouragement, and frustration in the collective pattern of Indian thought. . . . Today a large majority of the Indians on the four Nebraska reservations exist in a sort of twilight zone between two cultures—they have lost the best of their Indian culture and have reached out to accept only the worst of the white man's culture.[74]

Bruce went on to provide substantial details regarding many of the apparent "social problems" that he claimed had festered on the Omaha reservation during the Collier era, including alcoholism, peyotism, juvenile delinquency, educational and health deficiencies, and breakdowns in marital and family stability.

Bruce's comments about the law-and-order situation on the reservation are particularly noteworthy. After first acknowledging that state and county courts had been exercising jurisdiction over offenses committed by or against Indians within the reservation since the allotment days, he went on to report that the burden of Indian law enforcement had been exceedingly heavy for both Thurston and Knox Counties. Most significantly, Bruce compiled statistics from Thurston County jail records showing that, from 1946 to 1948, while Indians had been prosecuted for 285 offenses, whites had been charged with only 162. Thus, he wrote, "Indians committed 64 per cent of the violations of law in a county in which they constitute only 20 per cent of the population."[75]

Prosecution of Indians, Thurston County, Nebraska, 1946–1948

Morals		Malicious destruction	
Adultery	1	of property	5
Fornication	4	Sale of mortgaged property	1
Rape	6	No-fund check	2
Assault with intent to rape	1	*Subtotal*	19
Contributing to delinquency			
of minor	6	*Juvenile*	
Subtotal	18	Juvenile delinquency	15
		Subtotal	15
Violence			
Assault and battery	45	*Miscellaneous*	1
Assault with intent to do		Traffic (miscellaneous)	8
great bodily harm	2	Vagrancy	1
Breaking and entering	12	Mentally ill	4
Burglary	9	Nonsupport	2
Robbery	3	*Subtotal*	16
Manslaughter	1		
Subtotal	72	*Liquor*	
		Drunken driving	8
Property		Furnishing liquor to Indians	6
Auto theft	7	Drunk and disturbing	
Cattle stealing	1	the peace	131
Chicken stealing	1	*Subtotal*	145
Stealing posts	2		
		Total	285

	Total Offenses	% of Population	% of Offenses
By Indians	285	20	64
By whites	162	80	36
Total	447	100	100

Source: Report of H. E. Bruce to John R. Nichols, Commissioner of Indian Affairs, Exhibit E, May 16, 1949, Records of the BIA, Winnebago Agency, Record Group 075, box 349 (92M007), file "Programs, Jurisdiction, 1949–52," National Archives—Central Plains Region, Kansas City MO.

Bruce also prepared and attached to the report an exhibit (see table) in which he categorized the Indian prosecutions by type of offense. He went on to suggest that most of the Indian offenses resulted from excessive use of alcohol and noted that bootlegging and the manufacturing of Indian "home brew" were particularly prevalent in the area. In a refrain that would become even more common after the passage of PL 280, Bruce reported that county law enforcement authorities were "seriously handicapped" in dealing with the Indian situation by a shortage of funds. Thurston County officials contended that from 75 to 80 percent of all funds spent on law enforcement were devoted to Indian cases.

In the light of those numbers, Bruce suggested that the county needed and deserved more federal assistance than the single Indian policeman who was then stationed at the reservation could provide.[76] Bruce recommended that two additional positions of Indian police be established and urged "close cooperation with county officers in a more effective enforcement of law among Indians."[77] Instead of providing more assistance, however, the federal government chose the opposite approach—proceeding to abandon the Thurston County law enforcement situation via the passage of PL 280. A bad situation soon became significantly worse.

2. Public Law 280 in Operation
and the Battle over Retrocession,
1953–1970

How this situation can exist in the United States is beyond me.

Alfred Gilpin (1957)

However bad the law enforcement situation may have been on the Omaha reservation prior to 1953, passage of Public Law 280 in that year only exacerbated the problem. The disastrous effects of PL 280 would include, not only a further deterioration of law-and-order conditions on the reservation, but also an increase in racial tension and animosity between the Omahas and non-Indians living in the area. Not surprisingly, a fundamental dichotomy exists between the Omahas' perception of the reasons for these problems and the perceptions held by non-Indian residents of the reservation.

From the non-Indian perspective, the root cause of the difficulties that followed the invocation of PL 280 lay in the lack of funding for the local governments that were required to assume criminal enforcement operations on the reservations. After August 1953, all federal law enforcement personnel, few though that may have been, were withdrawn from the Omaha reservation. Prior to the act, Thurston County was already prosecuting Indians on a routine basis for all nonmajor crimes, that is, those crimes not falling within the exclusive jurisdiction of the federal courts under the Federal Major Crimes Act.[1] According to Winnebago Agency superintendent H. E. Bruce's May 1949 report to the commissioner, there was only one BIA policeman serving the reservation in the years immediately preceding passage of PL 280.[2] This federal "force" was not increased between 1949 and 1953, despite Bruce's repeated recommendations for more law enforcement manpower. Several other sources likewise indicate that only one federal Indian officer had served the reservation before 1953.[3]

Despite this apparently minimal pre-1953 BIA presence, some records seem to imply that the "complete" and "immediate" withdrawal of federal law enforcement personnel from the reservation was the primary cause of the ensuing lawlessness in the area.[4] It is hard to understand how the removal of a lone BIA officer could have become the basis for all the problems that ensued. It is probably more accurate to state that Thurston County found itself significantly overburdened by the sudden unfunded *increase* in its law enforcement responsibilities on the reservation since PL 280 had expressly repealed the Major Crimes Act in the mandatory states and the county would now have to prosecute Indians for both major crimes and misdemeanors. Whatever the precise effect of the removal of that single federal officer, it is clear that the county soon found itself unable to police the reservation adequately owing to financial constraints and manpower limitations. Law-and-order conditions in the area quickly deteriorated.

Statistics and anecdotal evidence from various sources combine to paint a dismal picture of crime conditions on the reservation in the PL 280 years. In 1961, for example, the Nebraska Unicameral was told that criminal cases involving Indians in Thurston County increased from 249 in 1954 to 353 in 1958. Likewise, expenses for the county jail increased over 178 percent from 1950 to 1959. The Thurston County jail had lodged 93 Indians at some time during 1949; by 1958, that number had risen to 334.[5] In a July 1956 interview with the *Omaha World-Herald*, Thurston County sheriff John Elliott acknowledged that four murders had occurred on the reservation in the previous six months and claimed that in each case "the cause was drunkenness followed by assault and battery." He asserted that conditions had worsened ever since the enactment of PL 280 and complained that rising costs for the transport and housing of Indian prisoners had depleted county resources. No funds were available for the maintenance of a deputy at Macy or Winnebago.[6] In 1970, the Thurston County attorney would declare that total criminal cases handled in the county had risen from 380 in 1955 to more than 1,120 in 1970. He further noted that the county was spending $5.47 per capita on law enforcement, compared to less than $1.00 per capita in neighboring counties.[7]

Tribal officials expressed the generalized sense of discord and despair that pervaded the community. At the Aberdeen Area Conference in 1957, tribal chairman Gustavus White decried the "virtual state of lawlessness" that had existed on the reservation since the withdrawal of BIA law enforcement.[8] One year later, a new chairman, Alfred Gilpin, echoed White's comments in even more poignant terms:

> Public Law 280 has actually left our Omaha and Winnebago Reservations lost since 1953. . . . Ever since then we have had no law protection. . . . The Omahas and the Winnebagos pay tax on their trust land. It seems as though we should enjoy the same services as other communities. . . . The county should be able to give us a deputy on the reservation, which it hasn't done.
>
> We had some killings going on there, one right on Main Street, which could have been prevented if we had law and order. This is not exaggerating. It's exactly the truth. . . . How this situation can exist in the United States is beyond me.[9]

From the advent of PL 280 jurisdiction, Thurston county officials maintained that they were doing their best to police the reservation, despite extreme financial hardship and the federal government's complete abandonment of the problem. The county repeatedly petitioned the state for assistance, complaining that it "was short on money, had only one sheriff, and there had been a dramatic increase in crime among the Indian population." The state provided little immediate help. Attorney General C. S. Beck noted that Thurston County had been handling Indian offenses in its courts since 1875 and offered only the vacuous platitude that "the problem in Thurston County is not one of jurisdiction. The problem is to help the Indians, and by so doing to help Thurston County."[10]

By 1957, however, the state had at least recognized the existence of the funding problem. Governor Victor Anderson met with the commissioner of Indian affairs in Washington to seek federal financing for increased law enforcement on the reservation. Given the passage of PL 280 and Nebraska's status as a mandatory state, the BIA could not agree to Anderson's request. The commissioner did, however, commit to bolstering the federal programs relating to juvenile delinquency on the reservation.[11]

On his return to Nebraska, the governor asked the state legislature to address the problem. Anderson advised the Nebraska Unicameral that, because some Indian lands in Thurston County were exempt from taxation, "it is apparent that the Indian population of Thurston County assumes a very small portion of the tax burden of that County, although constituting about $\frac{1}{3}$ of the population."[12] The governor went on to report that, for the year 1956, Indians constituted over 84 percent of the total jail population in Thurston County (236 of 280 individual incarcerations) and that the total annual cost to the county for the housing of all prisoners had been $10,549. To remedy the problem, Anderson introduced legislation designed to "equitably distribute the added burden of law enforcement imposed upon certain counties by reason of the passage of Public Law 280."[13] The bill, which passed into law on June 21, 1957, provided that the state would reimburse the county for expenses in excess of $500 per month incurred in the feeding of Indian prisoners, with the state commitment limited to a maximum of $500 each month.[14]

Within several years, it became apparent that the state's $500 monthly contribution would not suffice. On May 18, 1961, the Government and Military Affairs Committee of the Nebraska Legislature conducted a hearing to consider Legislative Bill (LB) 713, a bill that would amend the 1957 legislation so as to provide funding for up to three additional deputy state sheriffs in the counties affected by PL 280 jurisdiction. At the hearing, testimony was taken from state and local officials as well as from both white and Indian residents of Thurston County.

Norman Otto, appearing as the representative of Frank Morrison, then governor, expressed the administration's frustration with the PL 280 scheme. Responding to a state legislator who asked, "Why [is] this a state concern rather than a national concern?" (a question that in itself reflects the lack of awareness among state officials of the effect of PL 280 even eight years after its passage!), Otto replied: "Well, it is only a State concern because the State accepted the responsibility. It used to be a national concern, and they asked the State, would you like this problem, would you like to accept it, and the State said yes. ... Maybe the people made a mistake in 1953 but this was their decision. I think you're right. It should have stayed a federal problem."[15]

W. Earl Dyer Jr., executive editor of the *Lincoln Star,* testified at the hearing "as a private citizen interested in a problem on which the state must act." He appeared to have studied the Thurston County situation extensively and argued that the state had "the moral and legal responsibility to see to it that law and order is established in Thurston County—and that this blemish is removed from the political face of the state."[16]

Omaha tribal representatives presented similar appeals for state action. Council chairman Alfred W. Gilpin first rebutted the prevalent notion that the tribe was not paying its fair share of the financial burden in the county, contending that the Omahas had in fact been paying taxes on their allotted lands since 1910.[17] He went on to urge the committee to consider the proposed legislation so as to end the lawlessness "that has caused us to even lose some of our members by death."[18]

Tribal member Edward Cline likewise urged the committee members to take action, contending that the reservation was not safe for women or children at any hour of the day. The Reverend Reuben H. Ten Haken, a tribal member and clergyman from Macy, offered a particularly eloquent plea for state attention to the problem: "The Omaha Reservation is desperately in need of the kind of law enforcement that this bill makes possible. . . . We can testify to experience after experience that cries out for justice. . . . I visit people in the hospital monthly and sometimes weekly who have been knifed [or] beaten. . . . Violence and brutality are often left unreported. . . . Our community [has become] a haven for the lawless to ply their trades at the expense of ruined lives."[19]

LB 713 passed into law on July 1, 1961. As ultimately enacted, the bill authorized the governor to appoint up to three deputy state sheriffs for each county in which 60 percent or more of the persons convicted for violation of state criminal laws were Indians. The "60 percent rule" was a last-minute insertion in the bill, designed to accommodate legislators from northern Nebraska counties bordering on the Sioux reservations in South Dakota, who claimed that their counties were experiencing Indian problems comparable to those in Thurston County. The unanticipated result of that hasty amendment, however, was to turn what had been a well-intentioned measure into an "Indian Bounty Act."[20] Indians and their supporters contended that county officials now believed that the most expedient method to obtain increased state funding was to arrest more and more Indians. The resulting deluge of Indian arrests created great resentment among the Omahas, many of whom had originally supported the legislation.[21] The tribe became increasingly anxious to find some mechanism to escape from state jurisdiction.

Many observers believed that the lawlessness on the reservation in the years after the passage of PL 280 was exacerbated by the enactment of federal legislation in 1955 that permitted the sale of alcoholic beverages to Indians. Thurston County sheriff John Elliott, Walthill mayor Dale French, and other non-Indian officials repeatedly cited alcohol consumption as a major factor in the escalation of crime on the reservation.[22] At least a few Omahas shared Elliott and French's opinion on the alcohol issue. An article in the July 1, 1956, *Omaha World-Herald Magazine* quoted an unidentified member of the Omaha Tribal Council as asserting that the lifting of the prohibition on the sale of alcohol to the Indians had been the "worst mistake the Government and State ever made."[23]

In the minds of most Omahas, however, the problems in the implementation of PL 280 jurisdiction were not caused primarily by the increased availability of alcohol on the reservation or by a lack of funding. Rather, the general perception of the Omahas was that, owing to inherent racism and discrimination, local government officials lacked the fundamental *will* to police the reservation fairly and efficiently. Council chairman Edward Cline voiced that tribal impression in congressional testimony delivered years later: "[During the PL 280 years,] the tribe experienced harassment and unfair treatment at the hands of county law enforcement officials. . . . [We] were subject to physical abuse and discriminatory prosecution. Rehabilitation was nonexistent. Indians would be placed in jail upon arrest for minor offenses for which non-Indians would merely be told to appear in court. The county sheriff would refuse to set bail for an Indian, making him sit in jail until he could appear before the judge for arraignment."[24]

Cline went on to relate an incident in which a pregnant Indian girl had pleaded with her Thurston County jailers that she was about to have her baby. The baby was born in the jail, and the girl was given only an aspirin. Cline stated that, "as a result of this treatment, the baby died." Thurston County sheriff Clyde Storie strongly rebutted Cline's version of the story, contending that the woman had been found drunk in the street and was initially taken to a hospital. She left the hospital voluntarily and was later found again on the streets of Walthill. She was then jailed at Pender, where she could be monitored by a jail matron. A doctor was called and was present at the birth. The baby was born with the umbilical cord twisted around its neck and could not be saved.[25] Whatever the truth in this specific case, it is easy to envision the heightened tension and animosity associated with the incident.

The Omahas' frustration with and resentment of the state's exercise of jurisdiction under PL 280 lingered for decades. In an interview conducted in 1977, former tribal chairman Gilpin still lamented the tragic consequences of PL 280 on the reservation. He recalled his persistent but largely futile efforts to convince state officials to meet their newly accepted responsibilities to the tribe: "In Macy, we had murder, we had rape, we had bootlegging, we had gunfights, right on the streets. . . . I asked them, 'Why did you accept [PL 280 responsibilities] if you're not going to give us these services? . . . You're talking about money—we're talking about lives.'"[26]

As the situation deteriorated, tribal leaders, county officials, and concerned non-Indian residents took steps to address the area's problems. Realizing that it could no longer rely on the federal government for any substantive assistance, the tribe announced a long-range cooperative program for community development. The plan was designed first to identify the tribe's aspirations for its future and then to move toward those objectives with the assistance of state, local, and private institutions. As a corollary to its long-range plan, the tribe took part in a program administered by the national Association on American Indian Affairs called We Shake Hands. The program was publicized as an effort to "end the social and spiritual isolation of the tribal community by encouraging friendly relations between them and the white communities around them."[27]

On December 3–4, 1958, a conference was convened at which state, county, and tribal representatives sought to solve the law enforcement problems on the reservation. Although the tone of the meeting was apparently cordial and constructive, little substantive progress was made. Governor Anderson's representative at the conference was particularly passive, suggesting that the state would get actively involved in the problem only after the tribal councils and local officials had made "an honest effort" to solve the difficulties on their own.[28]

Despite the good intentions evinced, these conferences and programs could not resolve the day-to-day problems of law enforcement on the reservation. Less than a decade after the passage of PL 280, the Omaha reservation had gained a national reputation as a glaringly bad example of the inherent folly of the terminationist ideology in general and of PL 280 in particular. In 1957, LaVerne Madigan, executive director of the Association on American Indian Affairs, cited the Omaha reservation as a particularly heinous example of the disastrous effects of the PL 280 and terminationist ideology. In an article published by the association, Madigan wrote, "There has been no law enforcement on the Omaha Reservation since 1953 when, under Public Law 280, the responsibility for this passed from the federal government to the state of Nebraska."[29] Using more graphic language, Representative Arnold Olsen of Montana called specific attention to the Nebraska debacle several years later, declaring on the floor of the House of Representatives that PL 280 had created a "lawless area" in which "murdered men have lain in the street within the Omaha Reservation for over 24 hours before police have investigated."[30]

As the PL 280 years dragged on, the community-action programs and cooperative ventures ground to a standstill owing to suspicions and resentment among both the Omahas and the non-Indian residents of Thurston County. On July 25, 1969, tensions that had already neared the boiling point were ignited by an ugly incident in which a twenty-year-old white woman was abducted and raped by seven Indian men after attending the Winnebago powwow on the reservation.[31] Although the suspects were arrested and charged almost immediately, many non-Indian area residents claimed that the Indian suspects had been given preferential treatment. A letter signed by sixty-seven persons identified only as "concerned citizens of Thurston County" was mailed to local newspapers, alleging that the crime had been "hushed up" by local authorities. The letter, printed in its entirety on the front page of the *Pender Times*, starkly reveals the simmering racial tension and hostility that had festered in the area throughout the PL 280 years:

> We have watched the newspapers and listened to the newscasts since [the abduction and rape] happened and have seen or heard no mention of this crime. Why? A similar incident happened a few weeks earlier where two couples were beaten . . . and no mention of this was ever made public. And I would guess that the criminals were gently reprimanded and reminded that this was a "no-no" and that the Great White Father who doles out the monthly checks and commodities for this "poor" misguided minority group was unhappy with them. But they received their checks the next month so they could stay drunk and continue their drunkedness and criminal acts.
>
> We who live in this community are getting just about all we can take of this favoritism; it is time we whites demand our equal rights. If seven white men had committed this horrendous crime . . . it would be in the headlines the following morning and swift legal action would be taken.[32]

County officials denied the allegations of preferential treatment for the Indian suspects, pointing out that the crime had been reported in several area newspapers and on local television broadcasts even before the letter was published. Thurston County attorney Mark Fuhrman did acknowledge, however, that some areas around Macy and Winnebago were a "jungle," where it was not safe for persons to go out at night.[33] Once again, Fuhrman and other county officials pointed to the lack of state and federal financial support as the fundamental impediment to improved law enforcement.

The letter outraged the Omahas and Winnebagos, who called it a "slur on their race." In protest, the tribes initiated an economic boycott of white businesses in Walthill. The boycott resulted in a statement released by Walthill mayor Blair Richendifer in which most of the sixty-seven signers of the original letter apologized for any "misinterpretation" of the letter's meaning and contended that it had not been intended to condemn "the whole Indian nation." The Indians, however, refused to accept the proffered apology, noting that "it was addressed to no one [and] signed by no one" and contained "more of the same type of bigotry, racism and implications toward Indian people."[34]

Quickly, a county "human relations board" composed of both Indian and white representatives was formed to address the issue, and the boycott ended shortly thereafter.[35] As the seven Indian men accused of the crime were brought to trial in Thurston County district court, however, racial animosity continued to simmer. In January 1970, Anne Flicker, editor of the *Walthill Citizen*, reported that she had received a threatening phone call in which the caller invoked the name of the Omaha Tribal Council and warned her "not to come to Macy but to stay in Walthill like the other Walthill garbage."[36] The following month, Indian inmates in the Thurston County jail revolted against the overcrowded conditions there, threatening to burn the jail down.[37] Sheriff Clyde Storie called for assistance from neighboring law enforcement agencies and reported that force was used on at least one prisoner in quelling the disturbance. Several days later, three fires were set in Macy by arsonists, and Indian residents went to the streets to patrol the area.[38]

Ultimately, all seven of the Indian men accused of the kidnapping and rape were tried and convicted of crimes arising out of this incident. Only two, however, were convicted of the most serious charges of kidnapping and rape.[39] Those two men, Wayne Goham and Dennis Tyndall, were sentenced to life imprisonment, thereby producing more claims of racial discrimination. Wayne Tyndall, secretary of the Omaha tribe and brother of one of the men sentenced to life, claimed, "No Indian can receive a fair trial in Thurston County." Tribal chairman Edward Cline was even more vehement in echoing Tyndall's allegations of discrimination: "What we see is what we've seen from the beginning, the white man's intent to keep the Indian prisoner in his own land. . . . We know damn good and well our people don't get fair and humane treatment. . . . White law enforcement leans on the Indian. . . . We'll always mistrust the white man. We're not prejudiced against him. We're simply telling the truth. White people have to be watched. The white man has no logical reason for telling his children to watch us. But we have to tell our children to watch them."[40]

The non-Indian response to such comments was again voiced by Anne Flicker. The *Walthill Citizen*'s editor argued that the Indians' claims of inequitable treatment were "overexaggerated," stating, "It's been blown past the point where it's believable. I know they have been taken in the past. Now that is over and done with. Don't forget, a few whites lost their scalps, too."[41]

While incidents like the 1969 rape case served to escalate the racial tensions on and around the Omaha reservation, a more fundamental dispute between the Omahas and non-Indian residents centered on the question of how best to *resolve* the problem of lawlessness on the reservation—a problem that both sides readily acknowledged. This battle would focus on the concept of *retrocession*, and it became a struggle that the Omahas would eventually win.

By the mid-1960s, the terminationist ideology of the immediate post–World War II era was on the wane. Dissatisfaction with the effects of PL 280 in several states, coupled with the well-publicized failures of the Menominee and Klamath reservation terminations, combined to bring about yet another federal reexamination of the Indian jurisdictional problem. The new federal posture on Indian matters eventually manifested itself in Titles II–VII of the Civil Rights Act of 1968. Those statutes would substantially amend the provisions of PL 280, bringing dramatic changes to the Omaha reservation.

The process that would lead to the 1968 amendments began in 1961, when the Senate Judiciary Committee commissioned its Subcommittee on Constitutional Rights to conduct an extensive analysis of the legal status and constitutional rights of Native Americans. Led by its chairman, Senator Sam Ervin of North Carolina, the subcommittee gathered testimony and evidence over a seven-year period. In June 1965, a delegation of Omahas led by tribal chairman Edward Cline testified before the subcommittee, expressing a strong desire for amendments to PL 280 that would allow the federal government to resume jurisdictional control.[42] The investigation culminated in a comprehensive report issued in 1966 in which the subcommittee concluded that PL 280 had "resulted in a breakdown in the administration of justice to such a degree that Indians are being denied due process and equal protection of the law."[43] The report recommended extensive amendments to PL 280, including provisions requiring Indian consent to any further transfers of jurisdiction and, most important for the Omahas, provisions for the retrocession of jurisdiction back to the federal government.

After several more years of legislative wrangling, the Ervin committee's amendments to PL 280 came to fruition as Titles II–VII of the landmark Civil Rights Act of 1968. These provisions would collectively become known as the "Indian Bill of Rights."[44] For the Omahas, by far the most significant change was contained in Title IV, section 403(a), which provided: "The United States is authorized to accept a retrocession by any State *of all or any measure* of the criminal or civil jurisdiction, or both, acquired by such State pursuant to [PL 280]" (emphasis added).[45] With this statutory language, Congress cracked open the door for Indians in all the PL 280 states to escape the perceived inequities inflicted on them during the fifteen years of PL 280 jurisdiction. The Omahas would become the first tribe in the nation to push through that door.

Just as PL 280 had not provided for Indian consent to the transfer of jurisdiction to the state, the 1968 legislation did not give Indians the power to initiate retrocession. The federal government was authorized only to accept retrocession "by any State." Thus, it was up to the state of Nebraska to determine whether it wished to return jurisdiction to the federal government. The debate on this issue would turn into a bitter contest, once again pitting the Omahas against county officials and their other non-Indian neighbors.

The Omahas, of course, had been seeking an escape from state jurisdiction almost from the moment PL 280 went into effect. With passage of the 1968 amendments, the tribe moved quickly to position itself for that long-desired release. Chairman Cline traveled to Washington to meet with the commissioner of Indian affairs on the retrocession issue. He was advised to file a formal request with the BIA, after which a representative would be sent to the reservation to assist the tribe in its efforts. At those subsequent meetings in January 1969, Cline informed the BIA representatives that the tribe wanted its own jail and court facilities and that the Omahas would expect the BIA to provide law enforcement coverage on the reservation until the tribe could establish its own police force.[46] On that same day, the Omaha Tribal Council adopted Resolution 69-33, formally proclaiming, with some understatement, what the tribe had felt for years—that the operation of PL 280 over the preceding sixteen years had "not been effective in providing adequate protection to the lives and property of the members of the Omaha tribe."[47] The Resolution went on to expressly confirm the tribe's strong desire for the return of federal jurisdiction and requested "urgent action" in furtherance of that goal.

In sharp contrast to the Omahas' perception of retrocession as the long-awaited deliverance from their problems, Thurston County officials and non-Indian residents viewed it as yet another impending blunder on the part of the federal government. They described it as a policy fraught with danger and destined to make a bad situation infinitely worse. Once again, the local non-Indian perception was that, if only adequate financial resources could be obtained, the state and county could quite adequately and fairly police the reservation.

Sheriff Clyde Storie was so distressed by the possibility of retrocession that he wrote a letter to President Richard Nixon arguing against the return of jurisdiction to the federal government. Storie contended that retrocession would be a major step backward for the Omahas and could lead only to grievous consequences for the entire community. He warned against the "creation of special agencies for any one group of people" and proposed a "simple solution to the whole problem." Storie's solution, not surprisingly, was for the federal government to provide the county with sufficient funds to police the reservation adequately. With additional financial support, the sheriff claimed, his office "can do the job and will do the job."[48]

As Storie's letter indicates, local non-Indian opposition to retrocession centered on the potential danger and inequity inherent in the presence of a "state within a state," complete with its own police force and tribal courts. County officials argued that the "checkerboard pattern" of Indian- and non-Indian-owned land on the reservation would make day-to-day jurisdictional determinations a practical impossibility for both county and tribal police forces. Moreover, local residents believed that retrocession would entitle Indians to take advantage of all the benefits of state citizenship with none of the accompanying responsibilities.[49]

With these strong competing viewpoints before it, the Nebraska Legislature stepped into the retrocession debate. Attorney General Clarence A. H. Meyer recommended that the Legislative Council appoint a special committee to address the issue. That committee held hearings on July 31 and August 1, 1968, that produced the expected differences of opinion between the Omahas and county officials. The committee also visited the Pine Ridge and Rosebud reservations in South Dakota, which were then under federal jurisdiction, to determine how those systems were operating. Finding that federal/tribal jurisdiction on the South Dakota reservations generally "worked well," the committee ultimately concluded that jurisdiction should be returned to the federal government, provided that the BIA agreed to assume immediate responsibility for day-to-day law enforcement operations on the reservation.[50]

The Council's recommendation, combined with the lure of the potential cost savings inherent in the abandonment of Indian jurisdiction, proved too much for the state to resist. On April 16, 1969, the Nebraska Legislature unanimously adopted Legislative Resolution 37, in which the state retroceded to the federal government "all jurisdiction over offenses committed by or against Indians in the areas of Indian country located in Thurston County, Nebraska, acquired by the State of Nebraska pursuant to Public Law 280 of 1953." The preamble to the resolution clearly indicates the cost-cutting motivation for its adoption, declaring that the assumption of jurisdiction by the state in 1953 had led to "steadily increasing costs" that Thurston County did not have a sufficient tax base to pay for, and noting that the state's financial assistance to the county had "increased each biennium."[51] Plainly, the state saw retrocession as an opportunity to rid itself of a messy and expensive problem, despite the strong misgivings of local non-Indian residents.

With the issuance of the state's offer of retrocession, the burden shifted to the federal government to act on the proposal. Executive Order 11435 vested the secretary of the interior with the unilateral power to accept or reject offers of retrocession on behalf of the federal government.[52] When the state of Nebraska tendered its offer, Secretary Walter Hickel responded by ordering yet another investigation of conditions in Thurston County. The BIA investigators who were sent to Nebraska quickly confirmed what had been apparent for years— that law enforcement conditions in the county were indeed abysmal. The BIA reports and memorandums stemming from those investigations are replete with the now-familiar litany of claims and counterclaims among the Omahas and local officials. For example, in an August 1, 1969, memorandum, Area Special Officer William F. Walker reported that, in his meeting with Omaha tribal officials, he had been inundated with details of discriminatory prosecution, inadequate and inhumane jail facilities, and generalized mistreatment of the Omahas by county law enforcement officers. County officials, on the other hand, renewed their argument that they were willing to deliver adequate policing of the reservation if sufficient funding could be provided.[53]

In the meantime, yet another new phase had arrived in the continuing ebb and flow of federal Indian policy. On March 6, 1968, President Lyndon Johnson sent to Congress a speech entitled "The Forgotten American."[54] That message marked the Johnson administration's formal repudiation of the termination policy as Johnson called for a new policy of "self-determination" for American Indians. Johnson's new direction was embraced with surprising vigor by the incoming Nixon administration. The new president issued strikingly liberal expressions of encouragement for Indian autonomy, asking for, among other proactive steps, a specific congressional renunciation of termination.[55]

In keeping with this new policy of self-determination, and on the basis of the BIA reports confirming the poor law enforcement conditions on the reservation, Secretary Hickel ultimately decided to accept Nebraska's offer of retrocession. Yet a complication still lingered. The Winnebago Tribe of Nebraska, occupying the northern portion of

Thurston County (see map 1), did *not* wish to undergo retrocession, and it issued a tribal resolution to that effect on April 17, 1969.[56] Hickel attempted to meet the desires of both the Omahas and the Winnebagos by issuing a "Notice of Acceptance of Retrocession of Jurisdiction" dated October 16, 1970, in which he accepted jurisdiction over only a *part* of the area tendered by the state of Nebraska; that is, he accepted jurisdiction over only the area "located within the boundaries of the Omaha Reservation in Thurston County, Nebraska."[57] With that notice, the Omaha tribe became the first Indian nation in the country to undergo retrocession.

Yet, even before the federal acceptance, state officials had begun to express second thoughts about the wisdom of retrocession. Nebraska senator Roman Hruska and state attorney general Clarence Meyer asked the Department of the Interior to "take no hasty action" on retrocession until all aspects of the jurisdictional problems on the reservation had been thoroughly examined.[58] In the minds of state and county officials, the secretary's partial acceptance further complicated an already chaotic situation. Meyer contended that the state still retained jurisdiction to prosecute Indians because the federal acceptance of jurisdiction did not comport with the terms of the state's offer. Thurston County attorney Mark Fuhrman indicated his complete uncertainty over the jurisdictional status of the reservation, telling a reporter, "You tell me what's going to happen. I don't know."[59]

Despite the confusion among state and county officials, the Omahas were elated with the secretary's acceptance and proceeded with plans for their own tribal police force, jail, and court system. Congress appropriated $100,000 in interim funding to establish a BIA law enforcement presence on the reservation.[60] By late November 1970, a tribal judge, police captain, and five patrolmen were stationed on the reservation, awaiting construction of the tribe's new courthouse, jail, and police station.[61] That multipurpose building was completed in 1971, and the Omahas looked forward to a new era of self-determination and economic advancement.[62]

In the meantime, however, the federal government's partial acceptance of the Nebraska Legislature's 1969 offer of retrocession provided the state with a plausible legal theory on which to base its at-

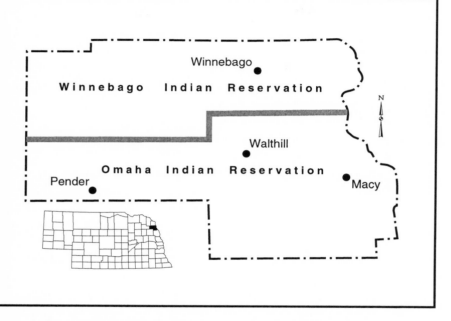

1. **Thurston County, Nebraska,** showing boundary between the Omaha and Winnebago reservations. Courtesy of Marvin Barton, Cartography Department, University of Nebraska–Omaha.

tempts to rectify what it now deemed to have been a mistake. Relying on the basic principle of contract law that, in order to be effective, the acceptance of an offer must be the mirror image of the original offer, the Nebraska Legislature purported to rescind its offer of retrocession on February 1, 1971.[63] The ensuing litigation over the efficacy of the federal acceptance and the state's rescission would once again lead to conflicting decisions by the state and federal courts.

In *State v Goham* (1971), the Nebraska Supreme Court sided with state and county officials and held that the secretary of the interior's action had not constituted a legally valid acceptance of the state's offer.[64] Rather, the court viewed the secretary's "Notice of Acceptance" as merely a counteroffer, which the state was then free to accept or reject. The court stated: "The measure of the jurisdiction to be retroceded was a matter for the state to determine, and is not dictated in any way by the federal act. The attempted acceptance was not in accordance with the terms of the offer, and was therefore of no force and effect."[65]

It is intriguing to note that, at least initially, even Commissioner of Indian Affairs Louis R. Bruce shared the state's belief that the secretary could *not* accept only *part* of the state's offer of retrocession. In an October 30, 1969, letter to Winnebago chairman Gordon Beaver, Bruce attempted to elicit a clarification of the Winnebagos' position, indicating that their refusal to accede to retrocession was a serious obstacle to the Omahas' request. Bruce told Beaver that Nebraska's offer could be accepted or rejected only in its entirety, writing, "We cannot accept more or less than the specific area . . . offered for retrocession by the state."[66] By the time of the secretary's "Notice of Acceptance" one year later, the Department of the Interior had either changed its opinion on this issue or decided to proceed with the Omaha retrocession despite it.

Notwithstanding the apparent strength of the state's legal argument (as implicitly acknowledged in Bruce's letter), the federal courts made short work of the *Goham* decision. In *Omaha Tribe v Village of Walthill* (1971), the federal district court held that the language of the 1968 amendments to PL 280 was sufficiently flexible to allow the secretary to accept "piecemeal retrocession." The federal court specifically rebutted the state court's reasoning in *Goham*, stating: "The problem I have in accepting the interpretation reached by the High Court of Nebraska is that here we are not considering a contract that was entered into between Nebraska and the United States Government, but rather a legislative Act. . . . The words 'The United States is authorized to accept a retrocession . . . *of all or any measure* of criminal . . . jurisdiction acquired by a State' refutes [Nebraska's] contention and gives the United States Government the right to accept 'any measure' of the jurisdiction offered back to it by a State" (emphasis added).[67]

The district court's decision validating the Omaha retrocession was upheld by the U.S. Court of Appeals for the Eighth Circuit in 1972.[68] When the U.S. Supreme Court declined to review the case in 1973, the Omahas' battle for retrocession was over.[69] For better or worse, the tribe was now permanently in control of its own law enforcement operations.

As might be expected, relations between the new tribal police force and Thurston County law enforcement officials were strained from the beginning. In its offer of retrocession, the state had retained jurisdiction over traffic offenses committed on public highways within the reservation. That loophole in the system became a particularly troublesome point of conflict between the two forces. County officials claimed that they were often forced to stand idly by and watch violators commit crimes because of the vagaries of the jurisdictional issues. Likewise, tribal officials complained that the county officers often acted outside their authority by making sham arrests for purported traffic offenses.[70]

An added practical problem for both police forces lay in the determination of the ethnic identity of criminal offenders or suspects. The newly created Omaha tribal court did not possess criminal jurisdiction over non-Indians, nor did it prosecute Winnebagos or other non-Omaha Indians who committed crimes on the reservation.[71] Just as many observers had predicted, this situation led to substantial uncertainty in the investigation and prosecution of crimes. Until the specific ethnic identity of a criminal offender or suspect was determined, it was impossible for county or tribal police to know which force had jurisdiction.[72]

On March 14, 1975, the BIA convened a meeting with tribal and county officials to resolve the lingering jurisdictional conflicts between the two police forces. The meeting seemed to swing toward the Omahas' view of the situation, with the issuance of a report by agency special officer Eugene Trottier in which he confirmed that various county police officers had made arrests of Indians for other than traffic offenses within the Thurston County portion of the reservation. Trottier's report further indicated that county officials were warned that the failure to coordinate their efforts with tribal police "might expose county officials to undesirable litigation."[73]

Several weeks after that meeting, Trottier wrote Thurston County sheriff Clyde Storie, offering to "cross-deputize" county officers so as to allow them clearer authority in dealing with reservation crimes. He asked that Storie, in return, offer cross-commissions as deputy county sheriffs for the tribal police officers.[74] Storie refused the offer, contending that the Indian police did not meet state qualifications for deputization.[75] County attorney Mark Fuhrman did agree, however, to "suggest" that the sheriff and his officers make a stronger effort to cooperate with the federal and tribal law enforcement personnel.[76]

Fuhrman's suggestion notwithstanding, the decades since the Omaha retrocession have seen continuing tension between the Omahas and their non-Indian neighbors regarding law enforcement and jurisdictional issues. By 1975, when the Winnebago tribe decided that it, too, wished to undergo retrocession, the state of Nebraska had concluded that the Omaha retrocession had been "a monumental mistake."[77] Numerous state and county officials journeyed to Washington to testify before the Senate's Committee on Interior and Insular Affairs, which was considering a bill that would allow Indian tribes such as the Winnebagos to initiate retrocession unilaterally. There, they related a litany of complaints regarding the adverse effects of retrocession and lobbied strongly against its extension to the Winnebagos.

The full story of the debate over the Winnebago retrocession is beyond my scope here. It may be noted, however, that the primary thrust of the state and county objections to the Winnebago initiative related to the perceived problems caused by the Omaha retrocession six years earlier. Among those testifying in opposition to Winnebago retrocession were Thurston County attorney Mark Fuhrman, Sheriff Clyde Storie, and the ubiquitous Anne Flicker, who contended that the Omaha retrocession had been a grievous constitutional error, inasmuch as it had the effect of "recognizing a sovereign Nation within the confines of the Continental United States."[78] In a less dramatic prepared statement, a staff member of the Nebraska Legislature's Judiciary Committee testified:

> The 1969 criminal retrocession of the Omaha Tribe was initiated for the sole reason of relieving the State of Nebraska of $90,000 of law enforcement costs. Since that time it has become very clear that the financial savings was of little compensation for the confusion and jurisdictional questions which have resulted. . . . This lack of clarity breeds

confusion to the extent that oftentimes jurisdictional authorities will ignore or avoid areas of unclear jurisdiction. When this happens, problem areas which otherwise may be resolved are simply not dealt with and the problem continues to exist or worsen.[79]

The non-Indian frustration with the "lack of clarity" created by the Omaha retrocession evinced in this 1976 testimony would linger for many years. Even nine years later, Sheriff Clyde Storie continued to insist that the Omahas "should be assimilated into the white man's culture" and that retrocession had been a "step backward" for the tribe. A local group of non-Indians calling themselves the Concerned Citizen's Council continued to complain of a "law enforcement void" on the reservation.[80] The gap between that view of the situation and the Omahas' perception seemed as wide in 1985 as it had ever been.[81] Captain Thomas Janis of the Omaha Tribal Police Force claimed that retrocession was "working real well" and that crime had dropped on the reservation since 1970, with a corresponding rise in tribal self-esteem and satisfaction.[82]

Janis's 1985 comments echoed the sentiments expressed by tribal chairman Edward Cline some ten years earlier. Cline had also testified in the 1975–76 Senate hearings, and his view of the situation contrasted sharply with those of the non-Indian witnesses. He asserted that retrocession had been a godsend for the tribe, allowing its members to escape "physical abuse and discriminatory prosecution" at the hands of county law enforcement officials. Cline concluded his Senate testimony by stating: "Although problems do exist, the Omaha Tribe has been very content with its law and order system since retrocession of criminal jurisdiction. Located in a Public Law 280 state, retrocession of criminal jurisdiction and the maintenance of the law and order system has been *the first step to self-determination* for the Omaha Tribe" (emphasis added).[83] That tentative and troublesome "first step" would be followed by more confident Omaha strides on different legal fronts in the ensuing years.

3. The Omaha Experience with
Indian Claims Commission Case 225,
1951–1964

This is a turning point of my people and we demand justice
Gustavus White (1955)

At the same time as the Omahas were attempting to cope with the consequences of Public Law 280 in Thurston County, the tribe was waging an equally consequential legal struggle twelve hundred miles away in Washington DC. The forum for that battle was the Indian Claims Commission (ICC). Created in 1946 at the outset of the terminationist offensive, the ICC began its life as a curious eddy in the current of postwar federal Indian policy. The ICC's creators envisioned an objective, nonjudicial forum in which the nation's Indian tribes could obtain a swift and permanent adjudication of long-held grievances against the government. This new tribunal was designed to be largely free of the constrictive legal and political obstacles that had always delayed, and often prevented, the resolution of Indian claims in previous decades.[1] On its surface, the legislation creating the ICC seemed to produce just such an entity.[2]

As many commentators have observed, however, the ICC in practice did not live up to the lofty goals on which it was founded. The commission that had been designed to be streamlined and nonjudicial quickly assumed a decidedly court-like sluggishness, bogging down in many of the same adversarial and legalistic swamps that had plagued the judicial handling of Indian claims in earlier years.[3] Given the volume of claims filed and the historical complexities of the issues involved, the delays were at least understandable, if not always entirely justifiable.[4]

More disappointingly, however, the high-minded principles on which the ICC was ostensibly founded were undermined almost from the outset by the burgeoning terminationist ideology, as tribal claims became enmeshed with and co-opted by the assimilationist aims of the Truman and Eisenhower administrations. In his message accompanying the signing of the act, President Truman hinted at this dilution of the motives driving the ICC's creation: "It would be a miracle if in the course of [our dealings with the Indians]—the largest real estate transaction in history—we had not made some mistakes and occasionally failed to live up to the precise terms of our treaties and agreements. . . . But we stand ready to submit all such controversies to the judgment of impartial tribunals. . . . With the final settlement of all outstanding claims which this measure insures, Indians can take their place without special handicaps or special advantages in the economic life of our nation and share fully in its progress."[5] Truman's suggestion that the ICC's resolution of Indian claims would allow the tribes to "take their place" in society presages the evolution of the ICC into an instrument of termination. In practice, the commission became simply a liquidating agent—a necessary condition precedent to the federal government's getting out of the Indian business.[6]

The creation, operation, and legacy of the ICC have been thoroughly explored and evaluated at the generalized or "macro level" by many knowledgeable commentators, including Harvey Rosenthal, John Wunder, Francis Paul Prucha, Vine Deloria Jr., Wilcomb Washburn, and others.[7] These observers have generally concluded that the ICC turned out to be, at best, a well-intentioned but flawed and incomplete resolution of the Indian claims problem. At worst, it is viewed as a bastardized travesty of justice and another tragic government debacle in the field of Indian policy.[8]

While the generalized effect of the ICC has thus received ample scholarly attention, a relatively neglected area of inquiry is the localized or "micro-level" effect of particular ICC adjudications on the tribes that prosecuted those claims.[9] The story of the grassroots experience, in this case that of the Omahas, from the initial filing of their claim in 1951 until its ultimate resolution in 1964, provides an instructive illustration of the complexities involved in the ICC process and the effect of the commission's awards on a specific tribe.

Just as the relatively small and overlooked Omaha tribe gained modest notoriety as the first Indian group in the nation to undergo retrocession (see chap. 2 above), so too did their ICC claims produce a first in the commission's history—the "Omaha Rule" for processing proposed compromise settlements. The result is an Omaha imprint on the annals of the institution that makes its claim particularly worthy of examination. Moreover, the Omaha case study offers the opportunity to examine several other seldom-explored aspects of the ICC's micro-level effect—the divisive intratribal controversies over the distribution and use of the funds awarded and the way in which those funds were ultimately utilized for the tribe's benefit. For the Omahas, these "aftermath" issues were as much a part of the ICC story as the claims themselves.

An evaluation of the specific effect of the ICC on the Omaha tribe requires a brief review of the commission's enabling legislation and its statutory mandate. The broad language of the Indian Claims Commission Act of 1946 seemed to provide all that Indian claimants and their supporters could have hoped for. The legislation created a three-person panel (later expanded to five) that was authorized to hear and resolve virtually every conceivable type of grievance that any "identifiable Indian group" might wish to prosecute against the United States.[10] Specifically, the commission's jurisdiction extended to five separately categorized causes of action, including claims based on fraudulent or unconscionable treaty provisions and claims based on land confiscations without compensation. In addition, section 2 of the act, an extraordinarily open-ended catchall provision, allowed the filing of claims based on "fair and honorable dealings that are not recognized by any existing rule of law or equity."

The act specifically extinguished any statute of limitations defense that might otherwise have applied to such claims and allowed Indian claimants to hire attorneys of their own choosing to prosecute their claims. Section 13(a) of the act, a provision that reflected the desired "once and for all" nature of the commission's mandate, required that all Indian groups be formally advised of the creation of the commission, and it actively *solicited* the submission of claims.

The act's liberal jurisdictional provisions were significantly tempered, however, by the limitations of the actual remedial powers exercised by the ICC. The commission awarded only monetary judgments; it did not restore land to claimants. For many Indians, cash awards, no matter how substantial, were not a satisfactory recompense for lands wrongfully taken.[11] Likewise, very early in its proceedings, the commission determined that it would not award interest on the amounts found to be owed to claimants. Its ruling on that issue was subsequently upheld by both the Court of Claims and the Supreme Court and became a source of considerable discontent among claimants and their supporters.[12]

An equally significant restrictive element was introduced by the ICC's method of determining land claims' valuation. The commission took the position that it would award monetary judgments on the basis of the value of the land in question at the time of taking, that is, at its eighteenth- or nineteenth-century value rather than at the current market value.[13] Coupled with the refusal to grant prejudgment interest, this limitation meant that the final judgments awarded most claimants would fall far short of restoring them to the position they would have reached had they retained the land in question.

While each of these limitations on the commission's power was essentially self-imposed, the 1946 act specifically provided an additional "reducing element" in the computation of final awards. In section 2, the government was statutorily authorized to "offset" from the commission's awards the value of certain payments made to the tribes in the past. The establishment of the appropriate amounts of these offsets generated considerable controversy and delay in the processing of claims, as attorneys sparred endlessly over the details of government payments and annuities made generations before.[14]

The determination of land ownership and valuation some one hundred years in the past necessarily turned the ICC litigation process into an interminable battle among experts and spawned a symbiotic cottage industry in anthropological research, ethnography, and real estate appraisal. While the resulting documentation would provide a rich source of data for modern researchers, the laborious process of collecting and analyzing that material became a significant additional impediment to the rapid resolution of claims.

Operationally, the commission's consideration of claims evolved into a three-stage process. The threshold determination, generally labeled the *title phase*, involved the establishment of Indian ownership of the land in question. If that issue was decided in the Indians' favor, the case proceeded to a second stage, the *liability/valuation phase*. Those proceedings involved exhaustive investigation and voluminous testimony regarding the facts of the claimants' allegations and the value of the land in question. If and when the liability issue was established in the Indians' favor and the value of the property determined, the commission proceeded to the third step, called the *offset phase*. There the parties contested the appropriate amount by which the judgment would be reduced for payments made to the claimants since the time of the taking. Each of these stages in the process typically involved extensive evidentiary hearings, accompanied by the preparation and filing of countless motions, briefs, and proposed findings on behalf of the parties, and generally concluded with the commission's rendering of an interlocutory order resolving the central issue in that phase, that is, title, valuation, or offset. Each of those interlocutory orders, in turn, was often subject to motions for reconsideration or rehearing, creating further delay and expense for the parties.[15]

The fourteen-year history of the Omahas' ICC litigation provides a classic illustration of the bureaucratic delays and legalistic wrangling that became ingrained in the commission's operations. The Omaha saga began with the filing of the tribe's original complaint with the commission on August 8, 1951.[16] Assigned Docket 225, the complaint initially asserted a number of grievances related to the government's negotiation of various, unspecified treaties with the Omahas prior to 1854.[17] Specifically, the Omahas alleged that they had been induced to enter into those treaties and agreements through fraud and misrepresentation on the part of government agents. The tribe's attorneys couched their claims in language that would become typical of many ICC petitions:

(a) By failing to disclose and explain the true meaning of the language used in the treaties to those executing the same on behalf of the Indians . . . [who were] unlettered and unfamiliar with the use of the English language and not comprehending the full meaning of the language used

(b) By secret instructions given to the Commissioner sent to negotiate treaties.

(c) By special inducements of lands and goods.

(d) By promises given to the Indians that they would be permitted to remain in possession of the lands described in the treaty.

(e) By promises to permit them to continue to hunt and fish in ceded territory.

(f) By making consideration payable at the will and pleasure of the President and Congress.

(g) [By negotiating and executing the treaties with Indians who] were without authority of the tribe and acted contrary to the wishes and intentions of the authorized leaders and members of the tribe.[18]

In addition to those specific allegations of fraud, the Omahas claimed that the payments made to the tribe for the lands ceded pursuant to the pre-1854 agreements had "amounted to a small fraction of the value of the land" and were an "unconscionable consideration." Leaving no portion of the 1946 act unused, the tribe also attacked the treaties by way of a generalized invocation of the act's "fair and honorable dealings" language.[19]

Having set out their grievances with respect to the pre-1854 treaties in the preliminary paragraphs of their complaint, the Omahas then presented five separately stated counts in which they attacked the provisions of their landmark 1854 treaty with the government and their treatment pursuant to several subsequent agreements. The 1854 treaty was the major land cession in Omaha history and the defining moment in their future relations with the federal government.[20] By the terms of the treaty, the Omahas ceded to the government all their traditional homelands west of the Missouri River, reserving to themselves only a 300,000-acre tract that would become the Omaha reservation. In return, the government agreed to pay the tribe $975,739.54 and to protect the Omahas from the Sioux and other hostile neighboring tribes.

In Count I, the tribe alleged that, owing to errors made when their traditional homelands had been surveyed, it had not been properly compensated for all the lands conveyed pursuant to the 1854 treaty. Count I further alleged that the government had failed to prevent white encroachment onto Omaha land prior to the 1854 treaty in disregard of the promises made in prior treaties. Count II alleged that the amount paid to the Omahas for the portion of their reservation that was set aside for the Winnebago tribe in 1865 was unconscionably low. The tribe asserted that it had been paid $50,000 for 103,000 acres, amounting to 50 cents per acre for land that they now deemed to have been worth "in excess of $5.00 per acre."[21]

In Count III, the Omahas claimed that the government had failed to protect them from the Sioux and other hostile tribes as agreed in the 1854 treaty, resulting in the deaths of twenty-two men and the theft of at least 152 horses and other property.[22] Count IV again invoked the catchall language of the 1946 enabling legislation, claiming that the Omahas had not been dealt with "fairly and honorably." Finally, in Count V, the tribe sought an accounting from the government with respect to its performance as guardian and trustee of the tribe's funds, property, and other assets. In their prayer for relief, the Omahas asked the commission to revise all their treaties and agreements with the government so as to provide them "the reasonable and fair value of the lands so ceded" and to compensate them for the depredations of the Sioux.[23]

The filing of the original Omaha complaint in August 1951 initiated a two-year period of tactical skirmishing in which the attorneys for the tribe and the government exchanged numerous motions, replies, and other procedural documents. On October 6, 1953, that paper war culminated in a commission order requiring the Omahas to sever the allegations of their original complaint into three separately docketed claims.[24] In compliance with that order, the tribe filed amended complaints, entered as commission Dockets 225-A, 225-B, and 225-C.

Case 225-B became the "Winnebago cession" claim, essentially reiterating the allegations of inadequate compensation for the 103,000 acres ceded to the Winnebagos as set out in Count II of the original complaint.[25] Case 225-C was filed five years later, asserting the tribe's claims for trespass and losses from Sioux raids, and repeating the request for an accounting as previously alleged in Counts III and V of the original complaint.[26] Those proceedings meandered through the ICC machinery for years, but both took a backseat to the much weightier allegations of Case 225-A.

Filed on October 6, 1953, the Omahas' amended complaint in Case 225-A refined and greatly expanded the tribe's original allegations relating to the 1854 treaty. It would become the centerpiece of the Omaha litigation, engaging the services of dozens of lawyers, anthropologists, historians, geographers, and appraisers over the next seven years. The complex mixture of ownership issues, boundary determinations, and valuation questions presented in Case 225-A illustrates the complexity of the ICC's burden and offers a compelling explanation for the glacial pace of its progress.

Any clear understanding of the ICC's handling of the issues presented in Case 225-A must be based on an examination of both the convoluted provisions of the 1854 treaty itself and the prior interpretations of that treaty by the Court of Claims and the Supreme Court. Pursuant to Article I of the 1854 treaty, the Omahas ceded to the federal government all their ancestral homelands located west of the Missouri River and "south of a line drawn due west" from the confluence of the Ayoway and Missouri Rivers (see map 2).[27] The "Ayoway River" referred to in the treaty is the stream now identified as Iowa Creek, which empties into the Missouri River near present-day Ponca, Nebraska. The artificial boundary running west from its confluence with the Missouri became known as the "Aoway" or "due west" line. The ceded territory was bounded on the west by the so-called Shell Creek line, on the south by Shell Creek and the Platte River, and on the east by the Missouri River. The conveyed land totaled 4.5 million acres, for which the Omahas were paid $881,000, or 19.6 cents per acre.

By the terms of the treaty, the Omahas retained all their traditional lands located to the *north* of the Aoway line, *unless* they found those lands unsuitable. In the event the Omahas deemed those "remainder

2. Omaha Cession, 1854, as determined in ICC Docket 225. Courtesy of Marvin Barton, Cartography Department, University of Nebraska–Omaha.

lands" north of the Aoway line to be unsatisfactory for their permanent home, they were authorized to exchange the northern acreage for a portion of the ceded territory south of the Aoway line. The new location in the southern territory was to be no larger than 300,000 acres. If the Omahas opted to accept the southern acreage, they thereby ceded to the government all their lands north of the Aoway line and were to be compensated for that land at the same rate the government agreed to pay for the southern cession, with an offset for the 300,000 acres chosen in the south. Finding the country north of the Aoway line to be too close to the home range of their eternal tormentors, the Sioux, the Omahas chose to take instead a 300,000-acre tract in the Black Bird Hills area of present-day northeastern Nebraska. That property (less the portion ceded to the Winnebagos in 1865) became the present Omaha reservation in Thurston County, Nebraska.[28]

More than fifty years after the 1854 treaty, the Omahas had still not been paid for the additional acreage north of the Aoway line that they had ceded by virtue of their acceptance of the 300,000 acres south of the line. In 1910, they sought and received from Congress a special jurisdictional act conferring authority on the Court of Claims to hear and determine their claim for compensation pursuant to the 1854 treaty.[29] The Court of Claims ultimately held that the Omahas' land north of the Aoway line had totaled 783,356 acres.[30] On subtracting the 300,000 acres in the south that the tribe accepted for its reservation, a balance remained of 483,365 acres for which the government was obligated to pay the Omahas the same 19.6 cents per acre it had paid for the rest of the ceded land. The Supreme Court subsequently affirmed the Court of Claims decision, with some minor modifications, and the government ultimately paid the Omahas an additional $117,655.31 for this "excess acreage" north of the Aoway line.[31]

On the basis of that tortuous history, the Omahas' petition to the ICC in Case 225-A ultimately centered on two fundamental assertions: that the 19.6 cents per acre originally paid for their 4.5 million acres south of the Aoway line was "grossly inadequate" and "unconscionable" and that the Court of Claims judgment in 1918 awarding the Omahas that same 19.6 cents per acre for their "excess acreage" north of the Aoway line was likewise unconscionably inadequate. With that framing of the issues in place, the case moved forward into the first stage of the ICC process—the title phase.

The title proceedings began with an exchange of motions and briefs in which the parties debated the res judicata effect of the prior Court of Claims and Supreme Court opinions on the ICC's consideration of the Omahas' ownership of the land in question. In an interlocutory order entered October 19, 1954, the commission held that the Court of Claims decision in 1918 was controlling as to the boundaries of, the acreage of, and the price paid to the Omahas for lands ceded pursuant to the 1854 treaty.[32] It further held that the Court of Claims litigation had conclusively established the Omahas' "Indian title" to the ceded property *north* of the Aoway line and that the government was barred from attempting to relitigate that issue before the commission. As to the much larger cession *south* of the Aoway line, however, the commission held that the Court of Claims decision had *not* conclusively established the Omahas' title to the land conveyed. Thus, the Omahas were placed in the rather anomalous position of having to prove to the ICC's satisfaction that they had in fact "owned" 4.5 million acres of land that they had already formally conveyed to the federal government by treaty more than one hundred years before. Only after proving what the federal government had already implicitly acknowledged would the tribe be allowed to address the issue of the appropriate valuation of the property.

On September 27–29, 1955, an evidentiary hearing was convened before the ICC to address the ownership question. University of Nebraska anthropologist Dr. John L. Champe testified on behalf of the Omahas, while the government relied on the opinions of Smithsonian archaeologist G. Hubert Smith.[33] Both experts conducted admirably extensive research into the history of the Omaha tribe in the disputed territory, and they reached similar conclusions regarding the *facts* of the Omahas' presence there. On the *legal* issue of title to the land, however, they came to diametrically opposed conclusions. Smith concluded that "at no time after their arrival on the west side of the Missouri did [the Omahas] have *exclusive* control or possession of the area involved" (emphasis added).[34] ("Exclusive" control was the ICC standard for determination of Indian title.) Champe, in contrast, took the position that the Omahas had indeed established exclusive possession of the area in question since at least the 1750s and that they therefore had established compensable Indian title to the 4.5 million acres. He testified:

> [The Omahas] were free to move about anywhere within the area, except to stand off these raids from the Dakota, and perhaps the Pawnee, or whoever; but they had their farms near the various villages we have indicated. . . . they hunted from the village locations out along the southern side of the Niobrara into west and north central Nebraska, and the intervening rivers out along the Elkhorn.
>
> At no time that I am aware, has any of the surrounding tribes made any attempt to settle within the [4.5 million acres in question] and *I can only conclude that the Omaha used and occupied that area as they chose during that entire time.*[35] (emphasis added)

Also appearing on behalf of the Omahas were tribal council chairman Gustavus White and tribal secretary George Grant. Their testimony is a poignant reminder of the bleak conditions on the reservation at that time and the tribe's aspirations for a better future. White told the commission:

> I come here to represent my people in their thinking, and what they have in their hearts. . . . We hired these lawyers to fight for what we think is rightfully ours. And my people have prayed that they will be given . . . what we think is rightfully ours. And if we are awarded what is rightfully ours, my people want to use this to better themselves, educate our young ones, . . . and rehabilitate ourselves some way. . . . This is a turning point of my people, and we demand justice.[36]

Ultimately, the ICC agreed with Champe on the issue of Omaha title. In an opinion rendered January 18, 1957, Chief Commissioner Edgar Witt noted that, "under cross examination, *Dr. Smith agreed almost in toto to the facts and conclusions as testified to by Dr. Champe.*"[37] Accordingly, he ruled that the Omahas had established, by use and occupancy, their title to the 4.5 million acres south of the Aoway line.[38] The case then proceeded to the valuation phase.

Just as the title proceedings had turned into an ethnographic and anthropological debate between the parties' experts, the question of the appropriate valuation of the Omahas' territory ultimately centered on the competing opinions of the parties' real estate appraisers. On February 24, 1958, an evidentiary hearing commenced before Commissioner Louis J. O'Marr to determine the fair value, as of 1854, of the 4,982,097 acres of Nebraska real estate once "owned" by the Omahas.[39] As was the case at the title hearing more than two years before, the parties' experts presented starkly contrasting opinions.[40] The government's appraiser, William G. Murray, divided the Omaha tract into five classifications according to the quality and desirability of the land in question.[41] He then assigned a sliding scale of values to the various classes, ranging from $2.00 per acre for "choice sites along the Missouri and Platte River" to 10 cents per acre for "very poor land . . . not suited for settlement." Averaging his figures across the total acreage, he arrived at a value of 55 cents per acre, for a total value of $2,725,000.[42]

Naturally, the Omahas' expert, the appraiser W. D. Davis, disagreed with Murray's conclusions. During almost three full days of testimony that would create two hundred pages of transcript, Davis vigorously advocated a substantially higher value for the Omahas' cession.[43] Arguing that the Omaha territory had been considerably more attractive than Murray suggested, and taking into consideration comparable sales figures for a period extending some twenty years after 1854, Davis ultimately arrived at a value of $1.50 per acre, for a total recommended award of $7,437,100.[44] Thus, the ICC found itself confronted with two widely divergent expert opinions on valuation, with almost $5 million hanging in the balance. Not surprisingly, it chose a middle course between the two extremes.

In a decision delivered on November 28, 1958, the commission criticized the opinions offered by both Murray and Davis and reached its own conclusion on the valuation issue. Writing for the ICC, Commissioner O'Marr held that Murray's work had been too limited in terms of the evidence considered. Davis, in turn, was chastised for considering comparable sales and other valuation evidence that O'Marr deemed too remote in time to be relevant to the 1854 value of the Omaha cession. Notwithstanding its criticism of both experts' opinions, the commission arrived at a figure that was much closer to the government's position. O'Marr held that the appropriate valuation of the Omaha cession would be 75 cents per acre, for a total payment of $3,736,573.40. Subtracting the previously paid "unconscionable" consideration of $975,739.54, the commission ruled that the Omahas were entitled to an award of $2,760,833.86, minus whatever offsets were found to be appropriate.[45]

With the issuance of that order, the Omahas' ICC saga moved significantly closer to a conclusion. Although the troublesome question of offsets remained to be decided and the separately docketed claims in Cases 225-B and 225-C remained pending, the general framework of a final resolution was in place. During the six months following the commission's November 28 order, the parties exchanged motions and proposed findings relating to the issue of offsets. The Omahas stipulated to a small offset of $25,000 for unspecified prior payments, but the parties clashed over the government's claim for an offset based on the payment of $374,465 to the Omahas in 1926. That payment had been specifically authorized by special acts of Congress as interest on the Court of Claims 1918 judgment relating to the lands north of the Aoway line. The government argued that the payment of that sum had been a "gratuitous" offering to the Omahas, for which it was now entitled to a credit against the ICC award. The commission disagreed. On May 6, 1959, it held that the 1926 payment to the Omahas, having been mandated by Congress, was *not* "gratuitous" within the meaning of the ICC Act of 1946 and therefore would not be allowed as an offset against the $2,760,833 award. That decision became the final dispositive order in Case 225-A. The amount of the award to the Omahas was established at $2,735,833.86, and a final order was issued to that effect.[46]

In the weeks following the commission's May 6 final order, the government filed the usual complement of motions to vacate or reconsider, all of which were denied. On July 31, the government routinely filed its notice of appeal to the Court of Claims. If followed to its normal conclusion, that appeal, combined with the pending claims in Cases 225-B and 225-C (which had by this time evolved into Case 225-D), might well have extended the Omaha litigation several more years. Fortunately for both sides, that dismal prospect was averted. During the late months of 1959, the government and the Omahas took innovative steps to consolidate and resolve all the tribe's claims in one final compromise settlement.

On December 22, 1959, the government and the tribe filed a joint "Stipulation of Settlement" in which they agreed to a final compromise of *all* the remaining litigation between them. The proposal encompassed the tribe's still-pending claims in Dockets 225-B, 225-C, and 225-D and the government's recently filed appeal to the Court of Claims in Case 225-A. By the terms of the stipulation, the Omahas agreed to accept $2.9 million in full settlement of all claims set forth in Dockets 225-A–225-D, and the government agreed to dismiss its appeal to the Court of Claims in 225-A.[47]

The filing of that proposed compromise settlement presented the commission with a situation it had not previously faced in almost thirteen years of operation. Its handling of the proposal resulted in the enunciation of a new set of operational guidelines for the approval of such settlements in the future—a procedure that would become known as the Omaha Rule.

In a landmark opinion delivered by Commissioner Arthur Watkins on February 11, 1960, the ICC approved the proposed compromise settlement and praised the Omahas and the government attorneys for their efforts to bring the litigation to a conclusion. Watkins noted that the commission's operations had become intolerably slow, and he urged other parties to enter into compromise agreements as "the best hope for the early settlement of hundreds of claims still pending before the Commission." While encouraging the use of compromise agreements like the Omaha settlement, Watkins also professed concern over possible abuses in the processing of such settlements, abuses that might later lead to renewed Indian charges of bad faith or dishonorable dealings. To avoid such a result, the commission enunciated a set of procedural guidelines for the negotiation and approval of proposed settlements, designed to ensure "that the agreements are fair, understood, and approved by a majority of the Indian tribe members, [and] that the Indians will accept the final judgments in good faith."[48]

Specifically, the commission's new Omaha Rule required parties wishing to enter into a compromise settlement to comply with the following steps:

1. On behalf of the Indian claimants, the original compromise agreement was to be signed by the tribal council chairman as well as all the individually named petitioners and their respective counsel. On behalf of the government, the agreement was to be signed by the attorney general or his designated representative.

2. The parties were to file a joint motion with the commission, one setting forth the terms of the proposed compromise and requesting a hearing on the matter.

3. An open evidentiary hearing would be held before the commission.

4. At the hearing, the Indian claimants were directed to present as witnesses the tribal chairman, the tribal secretary, and any other individual tribal members who wished to appear. Those witnesses were to testify as to "what has been done by them or the attorneys . . . to acquaint tribal members with the provisions of the agreement." In addition, the commission would require the parties to offer documentary evidence in the form of tribal council resolutions approving the compromise settlement and authorizing the chairman to sign the settlement on the tribe's behalf. The government was required to provide a letter from the secretary of the interior approving the compromise.[49]

Finding that these procedures had been substantially followed in the Omaha case, the commission entered a "Final Judgment" contemporaneously with its February 11, 1960, opinion in which it approved the compromise agreement and directed the government to pay the Omaha nation the net sum of $2.9 million in full and final settlement of all claims it had asserted in Case 225.[50] On that same day, the commission issued a separate order authorizing the payment of $217,900.25 to the Omahas' attorneys and $17,313.96 to their appraiser, W. D. Davis, with both bills to be paid from the $2.9 million judgment fund.[51] The issuance of those orders brought the Omaha litigation in Case 225 to a close. A few procedural obstacles still remained, however, before the Omahas would collect their judgment.

Sections 21 and 22 of the 1946 act provided that final ICC awards were to be submitted to Congress for the appropriation of funds for payment. Prior to 1960, this had been largely a rubber-stamp process, with the judgment amounts routinely approved by Congress and deposited into the federal Treasury for distribution to the tribes under the direction of the secretary of the interior. Beginning in 1960, however, Congress took steps to increase its oversight of ICC awards, requiring special legislation for the payment of each judgment specifying the use and distribution of the funds.[52] The Omahas' award became ensnared in this heightened congressional scrutiny, creating another significant delay before the tribe could reap the benefits of its hard-won legal victory.

The ICC formally reported its judgment to Congress on February 23, 1960. Bills providing for the appropriation and disposition of the Omaha award were then introduced in both the House and the Senate, followed by a period of over a year and a half during which the bills were considered by the Senate Committee on Interior and Insular Affairs and the House Indian Affairs Subcommittee. During their investigations, the congressional committees sought input from the Interior Department and, more importantly, from the Omahas themselves with respect to the anticipated uses of the judgment fund. As with most other tribes awaiting ICC awards, the central issue facing the Omahas was how best to distribute the ICC award—through individual per capita payments or by "communal" investments in tribal programs and resources.[53] The heated intratribal debate on that issue would have far-ranging consequences for the Omahas, including intense factionalization between on- and off-reservation tribal members, a redefinition of tribal membership qualifications, and a dramatic turnover in the membership of the governing tribal council.

The Omahas' decision regarding the distribution of their ICC award came on March 8, 1961, when the tribal council unanimously adopted a resolution in which it approved the provisions of the two bills then pending in Congress for the dispersal of the Omaha fund. Those companion bills, House Resolution 5971 and Senate Bill 1518, called for per capita payments of $750 to each enrolled tribal member possessing "Omaha blood of the degree of one-fourth or more" and provided that the balance of the judgment fund should be used "as appropriate for the future economic security and stability of the Omaha Tribe of Nebraska."[54] On the receipt by Congress of the tribal resolution and a similarly favorable report from the Department of the Interior, the appropriation bills were consolidated and passed into law on September 14, 1961.[55]

The statute established a four-month period for the filing of new petitions for tribal membership, after which the applications would be examined by the tribe over a three-month period for approval or rejection. By January 14, 1962, tribal chairman Alfred Gilpin was predicting that almost three thousand members would receive individual shares of the judgment. Adult members would receive cash payments of $750, while the shares owed to children would be held in trust until each child reached age twenty-one. The balance of the judgment fund was targeted for economic and social improvement projects, to be determined by the tribe and approved by the secretary of the interior.[56]

In June 1962, almost eleven years after the filing of the original ICC complaint, the per capita payments were finally distributed to each of the adult members of the Omaha tribe. For most of the Omahas, this tangible reward from the long ICC fight was a welcome, but short-lived, benefit. Ed Zendejas, a tribal member who was a young child at the time of the distribution, recalls the general euphoria on the reservation as the checks were received: "My grandmother was practically throwing dollar bills out the window. The general feeling was 'We're rich!'"[57] The *Walthill Citizen* reported a "considerable increase in business activity" as many tribal members used the cash to buy clothes, furniture, or appliances.[58] Others paid off old bills or made improvements to their homes, and many parents indulged their children with new bicycles. Still others used their per capita payments for giveaways and other traditional Omaha techniques of building personal and clan prestige. Not all the recipients used their shares so benignly. One tribal member noted sadly that the distribution had resulted in "too many drunks."[59]

While the effect of the per capita payments faded quickly, the communal portion of the Omahas' ICC award was earmarked for significant, and largely successful, long-term social and economic devel-

1. **Omaha children** enjoying new bicycles purchased by their parents with part of the per capita distributions from ICC Case 225. Photo from *Omaha World-Herald*, June 17, 1962.

opment programs on the reservation. Among the initial projects utilizing the ICC fund were the construction of three new family housing units and the construction of a new multipurpose community building designed to house administrative offices, adult education classrooms, conference rooms, and a large tribal meeting room/gymnasium.[60] In subsequent years, funds from the ICC judgment were used, in whole or in part, for several other reservation projects, including a new water and sewage system for the village of Macy, a factory for the manufacture of hydraulic tractor parts, a tribal hog production facility, and the development of recreational facilities designed to boost tourism on the reservation.[61] The U.S. Department of the Interior would note several years later that it was "most gratified with the effects of the programming by the tribe for the use of the balance remaining after the per capita distribution."[62]

Shortly after the ICC funds were received, Commissioner of Indian Affairs Phileo Nash appeared at the Omahas' annual powwow and complimented the tribe on its handling of the ICC fund. Nash specifically praised the tribe's limitations on per capita distributions and the fact that $40,000 had been set aside for scholarships. He urged the tribe to safeguard the children's portions of the award and warned that those funds should not be disbursed "in the child's early years before the full educational requirements are known."[63] Even as the majority of the tribe basked in the good feelings generated by the influx of long-awaited cash, however, rumblings of discontent were heard from other quarters.

Although the tribal council's decision to approve the distribution plan established by the congressional appropriation statute was unanimous and had been reached at an open meeting attended by approximately two hundred adult members of the tribe, not all the Omahas were pleased with the dispersal program. Tribal members who lived off the reservation were particularly concerned, feeling that their needs and desires would not be taken into account in making final decisions regarding the use of the communal balance of the judgment fund. As early as October 1961, an off-reservation faction led by tribal member Clarence White expressed misgivings about the distribution plan, demanding that the council "recognize their problems" and prepare "a joint program . . . to coordinate the off-reservation Indian's development with his reservation brothers." Many of these off-reservation members argued that the entire fund should have been distributed per capita, believing that they would realize little benefit from the on-reservation improvements paid for by the undistributed balance.[64]

The tension and divisiveness escalated over the ensuing months. By October 1962, the off-reservation faction had become a unified and potent political force, which flexed its muscle in the tribal elections held on November 5. Voters ousted longtime tribal chairman Alfred Gilpin along with four other incumbent members of the council.[65] Ironically, the new council and its chairman, Louis Saunsoci, had no better success in appeasing some of the off-reservation members. One year after the election, a small group of Omahas living off the reservation was still complaining that they were being treated like "outcastes" by the council and threatening lawsuits because "you have [our] money and are using it without [our] permission."[66]

In addition to the acrimony created by the tribe's distribution of the ICC funds, the "one-fourth blood" provision incorporated into the distribution statute became a source of great consternation for some Omahas. As of 1961, approximately two hundred persons with less than one-fourth Indian blood were enrolled as members of the Omaha tribe pursuant to the provisions of the tribal constitution adopted in 1936.[67] Moreover, congressional investigators determined that an unknown number of descendants of the aboriginal Omaha tribe were *not* formally enrolled as members of the tribe but were nevertheless entitled to share in the judgment.

To bring closure to the issue, the appropriation bill authorizing the payout of the Omaha judgment called for the secretary of the interior to create a new membership roll comprising *only* those persons meeting the one-fourth Indian blood requirement. The one-fourth blood rule would then become the new standard for tribal membership and would be incorporated into the constitution by amendment. By endorsing this procedure through a March 8, 1961, resolution, the tribal council unilaterally revoked the membership of some two hundred individuals. The ousted members were not only eliminated from participation in the $750 per capita distribution but also deprived of the various other services and benefits available to tribal members. Some of those two hundred did not go quietly.

In August 1962, one of the former tribal members who had not been allowed to share in the ICC distribution initiated a protest movement among disenrolled Omahas, culminating in a threat to seek an injunction prohibiting further distributions of ICC funds.[68] Although no litigation actually ensued and the protest quieted rather quickly, the ousted members' lingering resentment coincided with that of the off-reservation faction to create an air of intratribal tension and division that would remain for years.[69] That lingering tension would be reignited several years later when the Omahas received another influx of ICC funds.

4. Round Two before the Indian Claims Commission—Case 138, 1951–1966

This may be one of the most nerve-wearing, difficult situations that may have ever come before the Commission
Lawrence C. Mills (1957)

The Omaha experience before the Indian Claims Commission did not conclude with the tribe's receipt and distribution of the funds produced by the settlement of Case 225. As that case wound its tedious way through the ICC's procedural machinery, the Omahas also maintained an active interest in another cause pending before the commission. That parallel proceeding, ICC Docket 138, would eventually be resolved in favor of the Omahas in a manner similar to the way in which Case 225 was. It would also produce many of the same consequences, both good and bad, for the tribe and its individual members.

As the docket number indicates, Case 138 actually commenced several months before the tribe initiated its claim in Case 225. On July 20, 1951, the Omahas joined with the Iowa tribe and the confederated Sac and Fox tribes (hereafter collectively referred to as "the Three Nations") to file a petition seeking recovery of the fair market value of the respective interests of each of the tribes in almost 10 million acres in what is now western Iowa and northwestern Missouri. While the Three Nations were copetitioners before the commission, their interests in the case were largely separate and adversarial. Indeed, the tribes would ultimately expend nearly as much time and effort in arguing cross-claims among themselves as they would in establishing liability against the federal government. Taken together, the myriad claims and cross-claims in Case 138 presented the ICC with so bewildering a set of historical circumstances that one of the parties' attorneys would describe it as "one of the most nerve-wearing, difficult situations to ever come before the Commission."[1]

Despite the complexity of the legal issues and the shared nature of the claims involved in Docket 138, the case would ultimately produce a judgment of $1.75 million in the Omahas' favor—funds that would both benefit the tribe and resurrect many of the same intratribal tensions created by the award in Case 225. Case 138 therefore represents a significant and noteworthy chapter in the Omahas' modern legal history, one that again illustrates that the ICC experience represented a mixed blessing for individual tribes.

In addition, an examination of Docket 138 is useful as a classic example of the laborious tasks often faced by the ICC. In this proceeding, just as in many others addressed by the tribunal in its thirty-two years of existence, the commission was asked to resolve a labyrinthine series of disputes involving the interpretation of treaties and agreements executed more than a century earlier, most of which were impenetrably vague and contradictory even at the time they were executed. Notwithstanding the many legitimate criticisms of the ICC and its operations, the commission's efforts to interpret such anomalies and to produce some measure of justice for the long-suffering Native Americans are certainly worthy of recognition.[2] Case 138 provides a particularly useful example of the expository role played by the ICC.

Omaha claims in Case 138 centered on the convoluted provisions of treaties that the tribe executed with the federal government in 1830, 1836, and 1854 as well as those of treaties negotiated with other midwestern tribes, treaties all regarding the same territory.[3] The procession of events began in 1825, when the federal government intervened in the warfare that was then raging among a number of tribes in the Upper Midwest, primarily the Sac and Fox tribes of the Upper Mississippi Basin and the Yankton Sioux of southern Minnesota. To give a greatly oversimplified account, the warfare involved incursions from the east by the Sac and Fox, and from the north by the Yankton Sioux, into the traditional hunting grounds of the less-aggressive Iowa, Otoe, and Omaha tribes in the area of what is now western Iowa.

Seeking to avoid future difficulties between the warring tribes, the federal government sought to construct an agreement that would "promote peace among the tribes, and establish boundaries among them and other tribes who live in their vicinity, and thereby remove all causes of future difficulty."[4] The resulting treaty, concluded on August 19, 1825, at Prairie des Chiens in Michigan Territory, established a southern boundary on Sioux territory, which would become known as the "Article 2 line," and acknowledged the respective interests of numerous other tribes in the lands south of that line.[5]

The Omahas were not parties to the 1825 Prairie des Chiens treaty, although their interests in the area involved in those negotiations would be expressly acknowledged by the federal government and by most of the other tribes in the ensuing years.[6] By implication, the treaty also recognized a Sac and Fox interest in the area south of the Article 2 line, although the Omahas would later argue before the ICC that the Sac and Fox had "no proper claim to the area" since whatever interest they purported to have acquired was based on conquest rather than aboriginal use as a traditional hunting ground.[7] In addition, the 1825 treaty committed the government to convening additional councils in subsequent years to establish specific boundaries for the various tribes' respective hunting grounds in the lands south of the Article 2 line. Those future councils would also obtain the assent of other tribes with interests in the area, such as the Otoe and Omaha, who were not parties to the treaty.[8]

The federal government took no immediate steps to convene the promised additional councils, and, predictably, new tensions arose between the various tribes in the area. By August 1828, a bitter dispute had arisen between the Sac and Fox tribes, on the one hand, and the Omaha and Otoe tribes, on the other. The Sac and Fox claimed that any interests that the Omahas might have had in the Iowa lands had been ceded to the former via the 1825 treaty, and they threatened war against the Omahas and Otoes if they continued to hunt in the area.[9] The Omahas naturally claimed that their historic interests in this land could not have been extinguished at Prairie des Chiens since they were not even a party to that agreement. Hostilities also loomed between the Sac and Fox and the Yankton Sioux, who also had not assented to the 1825 treaty.

In July 1830, the federal government finally made good on the commitment it had made five years earlier by compelling representatives of the Omaha, the Iowa, the Otoe, the Sac and Fox, and various bands of the Sioux to gather once again at Prairie du Chien. The ostensible purpose of that council was to resolve the lingering boundary problems among the tribes in the area and thereby "remove all causes which may hereafter create any unfriendly feelings between them."[10] That benign intention notwithstanding, the treaty executed at the 1830 Prairie du Chien council did far more than simply resolve intertribal boundary disputes. It resulted in the tribes' unknowing cession of the entire area in question in exchange for small government payments and annuities. This area would later be labeled *Cession 151* among government policymakers (see map 3).

The negotiation and execution of the 1830 Prairie du Chien Treaty, and the events that followed its execution, would become the linchpin of the Three Nations' claims in the Docket 138 ICC litigation. In their petition to the ICC, filed July 20, 1951, the tribes alleged that, from the outset, they had been intentionally misled as to the true purpose of the Prairie du Chien council. While government representatives purported to seek only peace among the tribes, their actual goal had been to obtain the complete extinguishment of all Indian claims to western Iowa in order to open the area to unrestricted white settlement. This subterfuge, alleged the petitioners, was consistent with President Andrew Jackson's aggressive implementation of the recently enacted Indian Removal Act of 1830, which explicitly announced the government's intent to remove all Indians from eastern lands and force them into unsettled western territory.[11]

Unaware of those underlying political motivations, the Omahas and the other tribes that gathered at Prairie du Chien in July 1830 believed that the meeting represented merely the government's "initial step . . . in discharging its obligations under the Treaty of 1825 to fix and establish boundary lines" and that "a cession of lands would not be required by [the government]." Interpreters were provided for the tribes, but the Three Nations would later allege that those translators were neither willing nor able to provide the tribes with the assistance necessary to negotiate on an equal basis with the government.[12]

The plan presented by government representatives, ostensibly de-

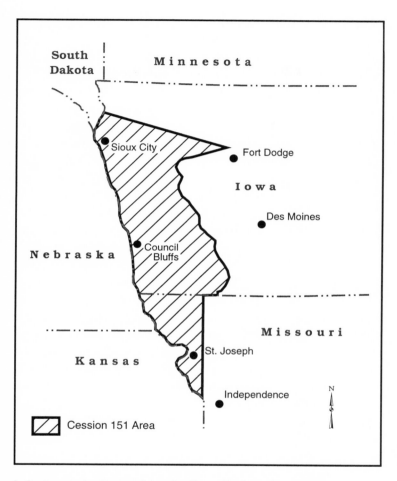

3. Cession 151 territory, as determined in ICC Docket 138. Courtesy of Marvin Barton, Cartography Department, University of Nebraska–Omaha.

signed to settle tribal boundary disputes, was in reality a masterful combination of strong-arm intimidation and diplomatic obfuscation. After first compelling all the gathered tribes to sign a peace agreement among themselves under threat of U.S. armed intervention, the treaty commissioners "proposed" that the tribes relinquish to the government "that portion of the country between the Demoine [Des Moines] and Missouri [Rivers], which you all assert a right to hunt upon; to be allotted as a common hunting ground."[13] This proposal would give rise to the fundamental misunderstanding on which all the later grievances arising out of the 1830 treaty would be based. The Omahas and the other tribes at Prairie du Chien believed that they were ceding the land *only* for the limited purpose of having it subsequently allotted and assigned back to them on the basis of fixed and specific boundaries. The government, in contrast, viewed the cession as an outright relinquishment of Indian title in exchange for agreed-on cash payments and annuities, with the land to be subsequently used and distributed in whatever manner the government might deem appropriate.

Specific language in the treaty can be utilized to support both viewpoints. The first sentence in Article 1 provided that the tribes "cede[d] and relinquish[ed] to the United States all their right and title to the lands [described]." A subsequent passage in the same article, however, seemed to place significant limitations on the government's future use of the land: "But it is understood that the lands ceded and relinquished by this Treaty, are to be assigned and allotted under the direction of the President of the United States, *to the Tribes now living thereon, or to such other Tribes as the President may locate thereon for hunting, or other purposes.*"[14] While the first portion of the italicized language was consistent with the Three Nations' understanding of the purpose of the treaty, they would later allege that they were completely unaware of the final clause in that passage, purporting to give the president the right to settle *other* tribes on the land in question.[15]

Laboring under these crucial misunderstandings, twelve representatives of the Omaha tribe affixed their marks to a treaty that would ultimately lead to the loss of more than 3 million acres of the tribe's traditional hunting grounds east of the Missouri River. The consideration paid to the tribe for this massive land cession amounted

to $2,500 annually for ten years, along with the government's prom-
ise to provide the tribe with one blacksmith and $500 worth of agri-
cultural implements.[16] The Iowas and the Sac and Fox received identi-
cal payments.

It took only three years for the confusion surrounding the meaning
and intent of the 1830 treaty to manifest itself. In a treaty executed
September 26, 1833, the government granted to the Chippewa, Ot-
tawa, and Potawatomi Indians a 5-million-acre tract that was entirely
encompassed within the Cession 151 territory.[17] That treaty was concluded without the consent or knowledge of the Omahas or the other
tribes involved in the 1830 agreement and without the payment of
any additional consideration to those groups.

Although that unilateral action by the government appeared to
indicate that the United States considered the land in question to have
already been entirely ceded by the Three Nations, the government con-
tradicted that impression by taking steps in the ensuing years that
partially acknowledged the *continuing* title of the Omaha, Iowa, and
Sac and Fox tribes. For example, in 1836, the government concluded
a series of treaties with each of the tribes that had been a party to
the 1830 agreement whereby the Indian groups relinquished their
respective interests in the southernmost portion of the Cession 151
territory—an area that would become known as the Platte Purchase
(see map 4).[18] The Omahas' share of the payment for this cession
amounted to just $1,270.[19]

In subsequent years, the government continued to acknowledge
the title of the Prairie du Chien tribes to the Cession 151 territory. In
1837, the United States concluded a series of treaties with the Sac and
Fox and the Iowa to relinquish their respective interests in the remaining area of Cession 151.[20] Likewise, in April 1838, the government acknowledged the Omahas' continuing interest in the Cession 151 territory by negotiating a treaty in which they, too, would have expressly
ceded their title to the area, but that treaty was never ratified by Congress.[21] Finally, in the seminal 1854 treaty that established the Omaha
reservation on the Nebraska side of the Missouri River, the tribe formally relinquished its interest in the remaining area of Cession 151 on
the Iowa side of the river.[22] The total compensation paid to the tribe

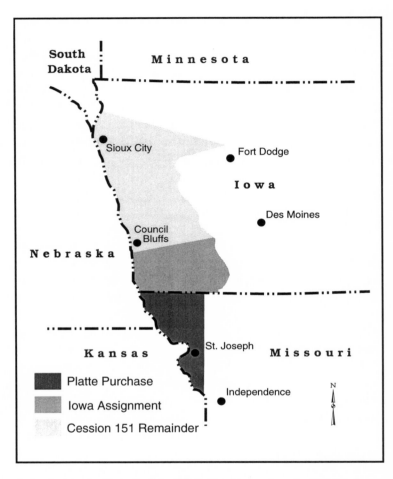

4. Cession 151 territory, depicting Platte Purchase and area assigned to Iowa tribe (Iowa Assignment) in ICC Docket 138 . The remainder was assigned to the Omaha, Otoe-Missouria, and Sac and Fox tribes, in one-third interests.

Courtesy of Marvin Barton, Cartography Department, University of Nebraska– Omaha.

over the previous two decades for the more than 3 million acres in question amounted to $26,270, or less than 1 cent per acre.[23] More than a hundred years would pass before that purchase price would be adjusted upward.

The ICC petition jointly filed by the Omaha, Iowa, and Sac and Fox nations in Docket 138 on July 20, 1951, took full advantage of all the potential theories of recovery provided by the broad language of section 2 of the 1946 ICC act.[24] In their first cause of action, the petitioners sought revision of the 1830 treaty on several alternate grounds: (1) that the treaty had been executed by the Three Nations under duress; (2) that the tribes had been induced to sign the treaty with the promise that the lands thereby ceded would be allotted back to the tribes with precisely defined boundaries; (3) that the provision in the treaty purporting to allow the president to settle other tribes on the land was directly contrary to representations made to the tribes at the council and to the tribes' understanding of the agreement; and (4) that the consideration paid to the tribes was "nominal in amount and unconscionably small."[25]

The tribes' second cause of action alleged that the government's acquisition of the Cession 151 area constituted a wrongful "taking" without just compensation in violation of the Fifth Amendment, for which the tribes were entitled to recover under clause 4 of section 2 of the act.[26] In their third and fourth causes of action, the Three Nations employed similar language to seek recovery under clauses 1 and 2 of the act, generally providing relief for all claims in law or equity against the United States.

Finally, the petitioners' fifth cause of action invoked the broad "fair and honorable dealings" language contained in clause 5 of section 2 of the act to attack a litany of government failings surrounding the 1830 treaty. Among these transgressions were the failure to provide competent interpreters and advisers and the failure to inform the Three Nations of the treaty provision that purported to give the president the right to locate other tribes on the Cession 151 lands.

After seeking and obtaining three separate extensions of time and being denied a fourth, the United States finally filed its answer to the Three Nations' allegations on June 2, 1952—almost one full year after the petition had been filed. The answer asserted the government's usual panoply of standard defenses, including the assertions that the government's dealings with the tribes "were at all times fair and honorable" and that the Three Nations had "received a fair, just and reasonable compensation for their purported claimed interest in and to said lands." More specifically, but no less predictably, the government asserted that the Omahas and the other tribes involved in the 1830 negotiations had not maintained the necessary "exclusive possession" of the Cession 151 area in the years prior to the treaty. Rather, the government argued that the land had been "used by numerous groups or bands of Indians as a common hunting ground and that no one group or band used or occupied the land to the exclusion of other groups or bands."[27]

In addition, the government took the unique position that the cessions of land made by the various tribes in the 1830 treaty were in fact superfluous inasmuch as the United States had already acquired full title to the area by way of earlier cessions by these tribes. Thus, argued the government, it had "acquired no additional right, title or interest in and to said lands which it did not already possess."[28] Just as in Case 225, the Omahas and their copetitioners would therefore be required to prove what the government had already explicitly acknowledged through its course of dealings with the tribes over several decades in the nineteenth century—namely, that the Three Nations had possessed both a de facto and a de jure compensable interest in the Cession 151 territory.

With the issues thus framed by the parties' initial pleadings, the case moved sluggishly forward through the title phase of the Indian Claims Commission's procedures.[29] After more than two years of reciprocal discovery among the litigants, the title hearing commenced before Acting Chief Commissioner Louis J. O'Marr and Associate Commissioner William M. Holt on December 7, 1954. Consistent with the typically glacial pace of the commission's proceedings, the witness testimony and arguments of counsel would ultimately extend over three separate sessions, spanning more than three years. The initial hearing in December 1954 began with the opening statements of the parties' respective counsel. The attorneys, including I. S. Weissbrodt on behalf of the Omahas, struggled to summarize the series of treaties involved in the case and the complicated web of claims and cross-claims. Just as in Case 225 and most other ICC proceedings, the battle among the experts then ensued.

To establish their title to the Cession 151 area, the petitioners presented the testimony of Dr. Anthony F. C. Wallace, an anthropologist from the University of Pennsylvania. Wallace testified that the Three Nations had each maintained exclusive occupancy of a distinct portion of the tract and that a reasonable interpretation of the provisions of the 1830 treaty necessarily recognized those respective interests.[30] The government countered Wallace's opinions with those of anthropologist and ethnohistorian Mildred Mott Wedel. Predictably, Wedel testified that the tribes in question had not established exclusive occupancy of the disputed area and that the treaty of 1830 did not give rise to compensable continuing interests in the land.[31] Following the December 10, 1954, session, the hearing was adjourned until February 23 of the following year, at which time Wedel concluded her testimony. The hearing adjourned the following day, and the paper war commenced anew.

For almost two years after the hearing, the litigants filed volumes of findings, objections, motions, replies, and other procedural documents with the commission. The countless papers exchanged between the parties during this period reflected both the emotionalism and the legal complexity of the case, not only between the government and the Indian claimants, but also between the claimants themselves. The written cross-attacks among the petitioners were, in some instances, even more bitter than the sparring with the government's attorneys, as illustrated by a set of objections filed by the Sac and Fox on December 26, 1956.

In the memorandum outlining their objections, the Sac and Fox attempted completely to exterminate the claim asserted by their Omaha copetitioners by raising the same argument that they had used against the Omahas in the years leading up to the 1830 Prairie du Chien council. They argued that the 1825 Prairie des Chiens Treaty had established the Sac and Fox and the Iowa tribes as the *only* owners of the Cession 151 territory. Omaha claims to the land, therefore, could be legitimatized only by "ignoring" the treaty or blatantly mis-characterizing its terms. By such misrepresentation, the Sac and Fox claimed, the Omahas thrust on the commission a "basic and material error" of such magnitude that it "raise[d] a serious question as to the adequacy and reliability of any or all of the Omaha's [proposed] findings."[32]

Notwithstanding such internecine disputes and cross-claims, the case was finally submitted to the commission for decision on February 15, 1957, following oral arguments of counsel. Six months later, on July 31, 1957, the ICC rendered its decision on the title issue. It was an unqualified victory for the Omahas and their copetitioners.

In its findings of fact, the commission expressly held that title to the Cession 151 area was in fact vested in the Three Nations, as well as the Otoe-Missouri, at the time of the signing of the 1830 treaty. It found that, by the pronouncements and actions of the officials conducting the 1830 Prairie du Chien negotiations, and by government actions following the execution of the treaty, the United States had acknowledged the use and occupancy of each of the tribes in the area in question.[33]

The ICC also agreed with the petitioners' arguments regarding the interpretation of the crucially troublesome treaty language that purported to give the government the right to settle *other* tribes on the Cession 151 lands. The commission held that the government's subsequent grant of land to the Potawatomi in 1833 was contrary to the plan under which the tribes had been enticed to execute the treaty. The area was being ceded to the government solely to allot it back *only* to those tribes whose interests were being acknowledged therein.

With the question of general Indian title thus resolved, the commission was faced with the more difficult task of establishing the specific interests of each of the tribes in the Cession 151 area. Writing for the unanimous commission, Chief Commissioner Edgar E. Witt noted, with justifiable regret, that the tribes' conflicting claims and the government's failure to abide by its promise to fix their respective boundaries made the problem "even more difficult now than it would have been at the time of the Treaties of 1825 or 1830."[34]

Witt ultimately held, however, that the evidence had established "with reasonable certainty" the parts of the Cession 151 area that had been used and occupied by each of the claimant tribes. The commission therefore proceeded to divide Cession 151 among the claimants as follows: The Iowa tribe was awarded an undivided interest in that portion of Cession 151 "lying easterly and southerly of the watershed which separates the Nodaway and Nishnabotony Rivers in said cession and extends from the Missouri River to the easterly line of the cession about midway between the sources of the Nodaway and Nishnabotony Rivers." As to the remainder of the cession area, the commission determined that the evidence was "not sufficient to make a division between the areas used by the Otoe-Missouria, Omaha, and the Sac and Fox tribes." Accordingly, it held that each of those claimants was entitled to "an undivided one-third interest thereof" (see map 4 above).[35]

After the usual motions for rehearing on the title issue had been filed and rejected, Docket 138 (now permanently consolidated with the Otoe-Missouri's claim in Docket 11-A) proceeded into the valuation phase. Almost four years later, on May 22, 1961, a hearing commenced before Chief Commissioner Arthur Watkins and Associate Commissioners William M. Holt and T. Harold Scott to hear evidence on the valuation question. The evidence presented in this phase of the case differed significantly from that presented by the appraisers in Case 225. While the petitioners offered the testimony of several experts regarding land settlement patterns, topography, climate, soil quality, and crop productivity in the Cession 151 area, none of those witnesses affixed a firm valuation to the land.[36]

The government, in contrast, again presented the meticulously detailed work of appraiser William G. Murray. Murray presented a 374-page report in which he analyzed the value of the land at three different dates.[37] For the Platte Purchase area in northwest Missouri, comprising 2,041,000 acres, Murray assigned a value of 50 cents per acre as of the date of the tribes' respective cessions in September and October 1836, for a total valuation of $1,020,500. For the western Iowa tract, comprising 8,338,260 acres, he assigned a value of 25 cents per acre as of February 1838, the date of the Iowa and the Sac and Fox cessions of that territory. For the Omahas and Otoes, he used a valuation date of April 17, 1854, and assigned a value of 70 cents per acre.

Unlike in Case 225, the commission was never required to render a final decision on the question of value in Docket 138. Led by the Omahas, whose pathbreaking settlement in Case 225 had produced the Omaha Rule for consideration and approval of compromise agreements, each of the claimant tribes in Dockets 138 and 11-A ultimately negotiated an individual settlement of their Cession 151 claims.

It is not surprising that the Omahas would have been the first of the Docket 138 litigants to seek and obtain a settlement. The tribe had received its long-awaited payment in Case 225 in June 1962, just one year after the valuation hearing in Docket 138.[38] As the 138 litigation meandered along with no end in sight and the Omahas realized the tangible benefits of their settlement in Case 225, the possibility of terminating their involvement in Case 138 in a similar manner no doubt took on increasing appeal. In the months following the May 1961 valuation hearing, the Omahas' attorneys negotiated with government counsel in an effort to reach a compromise regarding the tribe's claims. The negotiations reached fruition in early 1964, when the Omahas' claims were severed from those of the other tribes and the government agreed to pay the tribe $1.75 million in full satisfaction of its claims in Docket 138.[39]

With that stipulated agreement in place, the stage was set for application of the commission's recently enunciated Omaha Rule. This provision established procedural requirements for the approval of such compromises by both the ICC and the tribal membership involved.[40] The parties' efforts to comply with those requirements are reflected most vividly in the transcript of the ICC hearing conducted on March 13, 1964, at which the commission was asked to approve the terms of the proposed settlement.[41]

Appearing on behalf of the Omahas were tribal assistant business manager Francis Freemont Jr. and Wilson Wolf, secretary of the council. Both men were asked to relate the manner in which the tribal membership had been notified of the proposed settlement and the methods by which tribal approval had been debated and ultimately obtained. Freemont testified that a meeting of the tribal council had been convened on February 14, 1964, at which the tribe's attorney had explained the terms of the settlement in detail, to the unanimous satisfaction of the council. That acceptance was formalized with the adoption of a council resolution approving the settlement, a copy of which was offered into evidence before the ICC.

Freemont further testified that the council meeting was followed on the same day by a meeting of the general tribal membership at which the terms of the proposed settlement were again explained in both English and the Omaha language. Freemont related the steps that had been taken to give notice of the meeting to the tribal members, through mailings, newspaper notices, and radio and television announcements. Minutes of that meeting were offered into evidence, reflecting a vote of 228 to 2 in favor of the settlement. Both Freemont and Wolf were repeatedly asked whether they felt that the tribal membership understood the terms of the agreement and whether the members felt the settlement was "fair and equitable." Both witnesses consistently answered yes to those questions.[42]

In addition to its value as a demonstration of the Omaha Rule in operation, the settlement hearing in Docket 138 is intriguing as an illustration of the hoped-for finality of ICC decisions and the evolution of the commission into an instrument of termination.[43] The Omaha representatives were pointedly asked, both by counsel for the government and by Chief Commissioner Arthur Watkins himself, whether they understood that the proposed settlement would preclude the tribe from making "any further claims of any kind or purpose or nature against the United States." When Freemont equivocated slightly in answering that question, Watkins and the government's attorney took pains to elicit an acknowledgment from him that the time for filing claims under the ICC act had expired and that the tribe had no further pending claims before the commission. A similar acknowledgment of the finality of the settlement was elicited from Wolf.[44]

The terminationist flavor of the settlement hearing was even more directly revealed in the comments of Associate Commissioner Scott at the conclusion of Wilson Wolf's testimony. After being told by the Omahas' counsel that the tribe intended to distribute only a portion of the settlement proceeds on a per capita basis, reserving the rest for tribal programs, Scott remarked:

That is mighty good news. It isn't our objective here, but there was a hope in Congress that the settlement [of these] claims might have some influence in bringing the Indians into the normal cultural economic pursuits of life. I mean, they are mighty fine people, and [we need] any program that . . . gives them an opportunity to become assimilated in the formal pursuits of life.

We hope that eventually the Federal Government will be relieved of the present and continuing paternalistic burden, really I am not talking about finances now, but upon the approach, the Indians coming on out to normal life, standing on their own feet, and becoming leaders and members of the various communities throughout the country.[45]

Wolf and Freemont did not respond to Scott's encouragement of their future normality.

Satisfied with the evidence of tribal consent presented at the hearing, the commission entered a final judgment on April 14, 1964. It approved the compromise agreement and awarded the Omahas the sum of $1.75 million in final settlement for its ancestral hunting grounds east of the Missouri River.[46] Although pleased with the result, the Omahas' experience in Case 225 made them well aware that it would still be some time before the money found its way to the tribe's bank account.[47]

Just as had been the case with the $2.9 million settlement in Case 225, the Omahas were forced to wait more than two years for the receipt of this new award. By an act of June 9, 1964, Congress appropriated the $1.75 million necessary to cover the Omaha judgment.[48] Those funds were deposited into the U.S. Treasury to the credit of the tribe, to be held in escrow with interest at 4 percent per year, pending the preparation and approval of a plan for their distribution and use. On April 19, 1965, the tribal council approved a plan that, like the 1962 design, called for per capita payments of a portion of the judgment fund, reserving the balance for tribal economic development programs.[49]

On August 25, 1966, Assistant Secretary of the Interior Harry R. Anderson submitted a report on the Omaha situation to the Senate Committee on Interior and Insular Affairs, which was considering a pending bill for disposition of the Omaha judgment fund. Anderson's report provides an evaluation of the tribe's proposed distribution of the award in Case 138 and a revealing assessment of the Omahas' use of the funds awarded four years earlier in Case 225:

> In general, the membership of the Omaha Tribal Council has shown considerable sophistication in the management of tribal affairs during recent years. The experiences of the Council in the handling of programs established for the use of the previous judgment award has [sic] proven a valuable one and a number of tribal leaders show excellent leadership qualities. . . . The Omaha Tribe has made excellent use of most of the judgment funds awarded in 1960. . . . In general, it is our feeling that the Omaha tribal members have gained much valuable experience in the handling of their previous award which will benefit the program development of the present award.[50]

Anderson's report detailed many of the social, educational, and economic development programs funded by the award in Case 225 and concluded that the similarly proposed distribution plan for the Case 138 fund should be approved.[51] Despite the generally favorable tone of Anderson's evaluation, he stopped well short of recommending that the Omahas be given total autonomy in the use of their new judgment fund, and he made it clear that the Omahas' success in the management of the 1962 ICC award did not mean that the tribe was ready for termination from its federal connection:

> Despite the local activities stimulated by the use of the past judgment fund a great deal remains to be accomplished in terms of economic opportunities for the Omaha people. As was pointed out previously, the unemployment level and resultant welfare caseloads are extremely high. . . . Despite the forward strides being made it is our feeling that there must be additional time allowed for the tribe to gain the knowledge and experience which is vital and essential in the administration of complex tribal affairs. These qualities in the tribe must be assured before exclusive supervision and control of the tribal estate can be transferred to the tribe with confidence.[52]

On November 2, 1966, President Lyndon Johnson signed Public Law 89-717, authorizing the distribution of the Omaha judgment fund as proposed by the tribe and approved by Congress.[53] Seven anxious weeks later, on December 23, 1966, each adult tribal member received a check for $270. As with the 1962 award, payments apportioned to minors were placed in a trust account for future educational purposes. Shares were paid to 2,660 certified members, 1,279 of whom resided on the reservation. Not surprisingly, a portion of the money was used for Christmas shopping, but most Omahas reported that their shares went toward rent, groceries, clothing, and other necessities. One tribal official observed to a reporter, "You'll know when the checks arrive. The vultures [bill collectors] will be here first."[54]

While this additional ICC award was a gratifying and much-needed addition to tribal coffers, it also reignited many of the same intratribal controversies that had been smoldering since the 1962 ICC distribution. In the months leading up to the December 1966 distribution, an off-reservation faction led by Clarence White and Arthur Springer organized itself as the Land and Resources Development Association. The group leveled a series of public charges against the tribal leadership, accusing the council of establishing a "dictatorship" that discriminated against off-reservation members and ignored their plight in the urban settings of Omaha, Lincoln, and Sioux City.[55] The tribal council, chaired once again by Alfred Gilpin, responded to the accusations with an ostensibly sympathetic ear but claimed that the tribe's ability to assist the off-reservation members was severely limited by BIA regulations. Winnebago Agency superintendent Alfred DuBray confirmed Gilpin's assertions.[56]

The tension between the on- and the off-reservation factions would plague the tribe for years, resulting in sporadic intratribal political and legal upheavals following the final ICC distribution in 1966.[57] To a significant extent, those differences remain a problem within the tribe to this day as some off-reservation members feel a continuing sense of isolation from the decision-making process. Ed Zendejas, an attorney and tribal member who lives off the reservation, recently voiced that frustration, asserting that, "once you leave the reservation, you're ignored with respect to the use of tribal revenues."[58] That exclusion is grounded in the language of Article V, section 1, of the Omaha Tribal Constitution, which provides that only members who reside on the reservation may vote in tribal council elections.[59] Zendejas proposes that the tribe issue "ownership share certificates," comparable to corporate stock, to all enrolled members, whether they live on or off the reservation. Holders of certificates would be entitled to vote on a "board of directors" that would control tribal revenues in conjunction with the separately elected council.[60] It is uncertain when or whether such a proposal might be acted on by the council.

While such negative repercussions of the ICC awards should not be minimized, it seems difficult to dispute the conclusion that the ICC experience was a valuable one for the Omaha tribe. The funds generated by the two commission judgments were, by and large, put to beneficial use by both the individual members and the tribe at large. The educational, economic, and social improvement projects funded by the commission awards almost certainly would not have been possible without the ICC litigation. While it is a legal truism that justice delayed is justice denied, in the Omahas' case it may be argued with equal force that justice delayed is better than no justice at all.

Perhaps just as significantly, the successful resolution of the tribe's ICC litigation may have given it valuable insight into the rewards available to it on the judicial battleground. Even as it celebrated its 1966 ICC award in the new community building paid for by its 1962 judgment, the tribe was setting its sights on an even more ambitious legal fight. This would be a struggle in which the Omahas would seek, not merely monetary compensation for past injustices, but the actual reacquisition of land that the tribe felt still belonged to it.[61] The Blackbird Bend litigation loomed on the horizon.

5. The Legal Struggle for Blackbird
Bend, 1966–1995

The river will run red.

Albert Wood (1980)

Even a casual observer of modern Indian affairs is probably familiar with the Red Power movement of the 1960s and early 1970s. During that era, a number of loosely affiliated Native American groups known collectively as the American Indian Movement (AIM) became embroiled in a series of confrontations with federal authorities, some of which involved violent "self-help" tactics, and all of which garnered widespread publicity. Among the most notable of those episodes were the Indian occupation of Alcatraz Island in San Francisco Bay from November 1969 to June 1971; the "Trail of Broken Treaties," culminating in the occupation and destruction of the Bureau of Indian Affairs headquarters building in Washington DC in November 1972; the AIM occupation of the tiny village of Wounded Knee on the Pine Ridge reservation in South Dakota and the ensuing federal siege from February 27 to May 8, 1973; and, perhaps most tragically, the June 1975 shoot-out between AIM and the FBI at Pine Ridge that left an Indian and two federal agents dead.[1]

Less well known is the fact that, during this same era, the Red Power movement came to northwestern Iowa in the form of a remarkably complex legal struggle waged by the Omaha tribe. Beginning in 1966, the Omahas sought to regain possession of more than eleven thousand acres that the tribe claimed had originally been a part of its reservation in Nebraska but that were now on the Iowa side of the Missouri River owing to a shift in the river's channel. The ensuing legal fight in the Iowa state and federal courts, which became known as the "Blackbird Bend litigation," spanned almost two decades, ultimately producing a profound economic and emotional effect on both the tribe itself and the citizenry of northwestern Iowa. As the litigation wove its tortuous path through the court systems, the atmosphere in and around Monona County became so emotionally charged that one contemporary observer warned that the river might "run red" with the blood of the participants.[2]

Fortunately, that ominous prediction proved incorrect. No blood was shed at Blackbird Bend, but the fact that the river did not run red does not diminish the lasting emotional effect of the litigation on those involved. The legal struggle for Blackbird Bend generated feelings of animosity, frustration, and resentment that linger in some quarters of the region to this day, not only among the Omahas and their non-Indian opponents, but also between the tribe and its designated federal "representatives," and even on occasion among tribal members themselves.

Arising as it did in an era of particularly volatile Indian-government relations, when Native Americans were asserting their rights through increasingly strident and sometimes extralegal means, the Omahas' struggle to reclaim Blackbird Bend stands as a compelling case study in nonviolent Indian judicial activism. As the historian John Wunder has noted, the federal courts' treatment of Indian legal claims is a "story of continuity and change . . . that must be constantly told and retold."[3] The Blackbird Bend saga represents a noteworthy chapter in that continuing story.

The final outcome of the Blackbird Bend litigation cannot be captured in the simple terms of a legal victory or defeat for either the Omahas or the white Iowans who opposed them. While at first glance the twelve published decisions rendered by the courts seem to indicate that the Omahas succeeded in regaining their land, the tribe was in fact bitterly disappointed with the final outcome of the litigation. Theirs was, at best, another imperfect victory for they ultimately obtained title to only a small portion of the total acreage they claimed and they felt that they were the victims of fraud and breach of trust on the part of the federal judiciary and the Department of Justice throughout the proceedings.

90

Yet the Omahas' opponents could not be wholly satisfied with the legal outcome either. For the white farmers in Iowa who had asserted title to the land prior to the litigation, the loss of even a single acre was a bitter pill to swallow. Even those Iowans whose title to the property was ultimately upheld by the courts incurred substantial legal expenses and endured years of uncertainty as the cases plodded through the system.

The Blackbird Bend litigation received a great deal of contemporaneous attention in regional newspapers and the popular press.[4] Academic commentary on the matter, however, is relatively scarce and has generally focused on specific aspects of the parties' claims or the courts' holdings in isolated portions of the litigation. Notwithstanding those admirable examinations of certain parts of the story, the Blackbird Bend dispute as a whole has yet to be fully synthesized, and it remains a subject of national import on several levels.

Viewed from the most technical perspective, the Blackbird Bend decisions produced significant judicial statements on the arcane subject of riparian landowners' rights as those rights are affected by the complex geological actions known as *accretion* and *avulsion*.[5] In addition, the dispute required the courts to interpret and apply a federal statute enacted in 1834 that gave a clear judicial preference to Indian claimants in any boundary litigation with "white persons."[6] That statute had never previously been invoked or interpreted by the courts, and its constitutionality and applicability to the Blackbird Bend dispute became the subject of substantial debate, both among the parties and in the academic press.[7]

On another level, the Blackbird Bend litigation provides valuable insight into the often overlooked human dimensions of legal issues relating to land ownership. Both the Omahas and the Iowans pursued their claims with a dogged determination that occasionally approached violence, offering stark evidence of the deep emotional bonds that tie people to the lands of their ancestors. That emotionalism grew stronger as the litigation made its way through the court system, eventually overshadowing the staid legal concepts at issue in the cases. Indeed, the lingering discontent and resentment on both sides of the litigation are among the most troubling legacies of the Blackbird Bend saga.

Perhaps most significantly, Blackbird Bend offers an important opportunity to examine the localized effect of federal Indian policy, specifically in the context of the federal government's paternalistic and often troublesome role as the continuing trustee of Indian lands.[8] The court documents, transcripts, and other records pertaining to the litigation reveal an extremely antagonistic relationship between the Omahas and the government attorneys who were bound by law to act on the tribe's behalf. Throughout the proceedings, the Omahas found themselves "represented" by officials who did not share their view of the facts or the law and whose "assistance" the tribe would have much preferred to do without.[9] The Omahas' conflict with their purported trustee is the more obscure story within the story at Blackbird Bend—an extremely significant part of the picture that is not readily apparent in the published case law, the contemporary news accounts, or the academic analysis of the litigation. For the Omahas, however, those conflicts were every bit as much a part of the Blackbird Bend story as the court decisions themselves.

Although actual litigation would not commence until 1975, the Omahas began giving formal notice of their claims to the Blackbird Bend area as early as 1966. In February of that year, tribal chairman Alfred Gilpin first indicated that the Omahas had "staked their claim" to the Iowa land with Bureau of Indian Affairs (BIA) officials and that "action was pending" on the matter.[10] The tribe's stated objective was to gain official recognition of the land as a part of the Omaha reservation. That initial claim encompassed three full sections and parts of three others as the area was then platted by the state of Iowa.

From the beginning of the dispute, the Omahas' claims were grounded in the language of their seminal 1854 treaty with the federal government, in which they ceded the remainder of their traditional hunting grounds on both sides of the Missouri River in exchange for a 300,000-acre reservation in northeastern Nebraska.[11] The precise acreage set aside for the Omaha reservation was not formally established until 1867, when the boundaries were surveyed for the General Land Office by T. H. Barrett. The Barrett survey established the eastern boundary of the reservation as the "centre" of the Missouri River's main channel.[12] At the time of the survey, the reservation acreage *included* a thumb-like "meander lobe" known as "Blackbird Bend" jutting east from Nebraska toward Iowa. Over the next seventy years, until the river channel was stabilized by the Corps of Engineers in the 1940s, the river meandered back and forth over the Blackbird Bend lands, ultimately "straightening" itself to the west and south and leaving the Blackbird Bend lobe on the Iowa side of the river (see map 5). As that land was cut off from the remainder of the reservation, non-Indians in Iowa gradually took control of the property.[13]

In asserting its claim to those Iowa lands, the Omaha tribe swept itself and its opponents into a judicial maelstrom—one that would weave an incredibly complex trail through the federal court system over a period of almost twenty years. In addition to the Supreme Court's review of the dispute, the Eighth Circuit Court of Appeals would address the case on seven separate occasions, and the Federal District Court for the Northern District of Iowa would render four separate published opinions in the cases.[14]

The Omahas' "notice" to the BIA in early 1966 produced no immediate results. In December of that year, the tribe announced that the matter was "in the hands of their attorneys" for the possible filing of a lawsuit to reclaim the land.[15] Despite that hint of immediate action, the issue lingered for several more years while the tribe conferred with BIA officials and Interior Department attorneys regarding the details of their claim.[16]

In August 1972, Nebraska senators Roman Hruska and Carl Curtis, joined by Representative Charles Thone, delivered a letter to Indian Commissioner Louis Bruce asking the BIA to allocate $50,000 to help settle the simmering boundary dispute along the river. Bruce was advised that the Omaha and Winnebago tribes claimed as much as nine thousand acres on the Iowa side of the river, land that was "being used for private gain by Iowa farmers and the state government."[17] Before the BIA's bureaucratic machinery plodded into action, however, the burgeoning spirit of Indian political activism that swept the United States in the early 1970s found its way to the Omaha reservation, bringing the Blackbird Bend dispute to a potentially dangerous head.

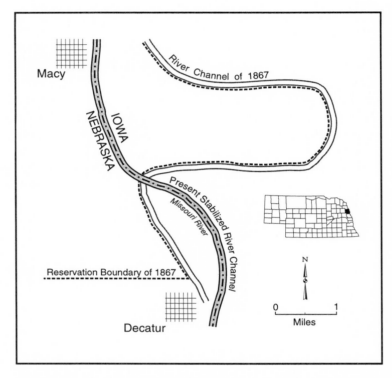

5. Missouri River at Blackbird Bend, depicting the movement of the channel from 1867 to the present. Courtesy of State Historical Society of Iowa.

On April 3, 1973, twelve carloads of Omaha Indians moved onto a portion of the Blackbird Bend lands in Monona County. Led by former (and future) tribal chairman Edward Cline, the "occupying force" pitched several tepees and tents on the land, announcing their intention to remain indefinitely and to farm the ground for tribal benefit.[18] They also brought with them, and displayed prominently for the local press who converged on the site, a large framed copy of the 1854 treaty on which their claim was based. Most of the group identified themselves as members of the American Indian Movement, an organization that had achieved nationwide notoriety in the preceding years as an aggressive instrument for the advocacy of Indian rights. Indeed, the occupation of Blackbird Bend occurred almost simultaneously with the resolution of one of AIM's most renowned actions—the Indian occupation and the subsequent government siege of the village of Wounded Knee on the Pine Ridge Sioux reservation in South Dakota.[19]

With the violence at Wounded Knee fresh in everyone's mind, the Omahas and local officials all expressed hope that Blackbird Bend "would not turn into another Wounded Knee."[20] Tensions ran high nevertheless as Cline informed authorities that, although the Omahas were unarmed, they would resist efforts to remove them from the land. Two days after the occupation began, the Indians met at the site with a group of attorneys representing the Iowa claimants of the

2. **Omaha tribal members** Mitchell and Matt Sheridan display a copy of the Omahas' 1854 treaty during the 1973 occupation of Blackbird Bend. Photo from *Omaha World-Herald*, April 7, 1973.

land. The thirty-minute conference brought no appreciable change in the parties' positions. The attorneys maintained that their clients had obtained title to the land through several "quiet title" actions prosecuted in the Iowa state courts in previous years.[21] The Omahas argued that those decisions had no effect on their ownership of the land since the tribe had not been named as an interested party in the suit and that the Iowa courts had no jurisdiction over an Indian reservation. The occupiers also told reporters that they would "defend our land the way you would defend your home" and blamed the federal government for failing to protect the tribe's interests as the land had slipped into white control.[22]

Several weeks later, Cline and two other men involved in the occupation were arrested on larceny charges by the Monona County Sheriff's Department. The arrests occurred after the men picked corn that had been planted on the disputed land by the Iowans.[23] While the other two men were released routinely on bond, Cline chose to remain in jail and was released five days later after a preliminary hearing. The charges against the men were referred to the Monona County grand jury to determine whether indictments were warranted.[24]

While those criminal proceedings were pending, one of the Iowa lessees of the land, Harold Jackson, initiated a civil action against Cline and the other occupying Indians to try to regain possession. The matter was heard on May 7 by Monona County district judge Donald Pendleton.[25] Nine days later, Pendleton issued an order requiring Cline and the other Omahas to vacate the land pending further hearings on the question of title to the property. This opening round in the fight for Blackbird Bend then quickly subsided as Cline and the other Indians left the property before Monona County sheriff Albert Wood arrived to formally serve them with Pendleton's order.[26]

The Omahas were not sufficiently funded or unified to sustain this initial occupation of Blackbird Bend. Because the AIM-sponsored action was not endorsed by the Omaha Tribal Council, Cline and the other AIM members were forced to look elsewhere for financial assistance.[27] When that effort failed, the occupiers retreated, but they remained committed to the goal of gaining the disputed lands.

Meanwhile, the BIA, which had been asked to address the matter more than seven years earlier, finally lurched into limited action. Wyman Babby, Aberdeen area director for the BIA, requested a formal opinion on the question of title from the solicitor of the Department of the Interior.[28] With the issuance of that opinion in February 1975 and a change in the leadership of the tribal council in the interim, the stage was set for the Omahas to return to Blackbird Bend.

On April 2, 1975, members of the tribe reoccupied the Blackbird Bend lands. Several key elements distinguished this effort from the short-lived 1973 sit-in. First, and most significantly, the 1975 occupation was fully endorsed by the Omaha Tribal Council, which was now chaired by the leader of the failed 1973 action, Edward Cline. Whatever AIM presence may have remained from 1973 was no longer visible in 1975, and the tribe presented a unified and cohesive front in asserting its right to the land.[29] Signs were erected around the property reading "Boundary line Omaha Indian Reservation. No trespassing. Federal law prohibits damage or removal of this sign. Violators will be prosecuted. Omaha Tribal Council."[30] The occupiers constructed a small heated cottage on the property and prepared for a long stay.

The 1975 occupation was also supported by BIA officials, buttressed by an Interior Department opinion in which the federal government formally asserted Indian title to the property.[31] That opinion, authored by Interior Department solicitor Kent Frizzell, declared that the disputed lands had been a part of the Omaha Indian Reservation since 1854 and that title should be vested in the United States as trustee for the tribe.[32] On the basis of that conclusion, BIA attorney Herbert Becker publicly reiterated the Omahas' original argument that the earlier quiet title actions in the Iowa state courts had not resolved the question of title to the property since neither the Omahas nor the federal government had been named as parties in that suit.[33] Beyond Frizzell's assertion of Indian title to the property, however, there was little agreement between the Omahas and the federal government on any other issue relating to the Blackbird Bend dispute. Indeed, from that point on, the tribe would find itself spending nearly as much time battling its government "representatives" as it would in fighting the Iowa claimants of the land.

3. Omaha tribal members outside the small cottage erected during the 1975 reoccupation of the Blackbird Bend lands. Photo from *Omaha World-Herald*, April 8, 1975.

The BIA's initial proposal for solving the Blackbird Bend problem suggested that the Iowans simply lease the land from the federal government as trustee for the tribe and continue to farm it as they had been doing during the previous decades. Not surprisingly, that proposal held little appeal for either the Omahas or the Iowa farmers. The Omahas did not want to lease to the Iowa claimants since the tribe's constitution mandated that tribal members be given first priority in the awarding of leases.[34] For their part, the Iowans expressed little interest in renting land that they believed they had owned for generations.[35]

Even if the Omahas had been amenable to the BIA's leasing proposal, significant disagreements remained over the specific manner in which Omaha title to the property would be formally established. BIA attorneys advised the Omahas that court action would be required to fully establish the tribe's ownership. They reasoned, quite sensibly, that the Iowa claimants would not agree to being ousted without first having their day in court.[36] Having waited almost ten years for the government to take action on their claims, however, the Omahas were in no mood to wait for the courts to grind their way to a decision in the case.

In a meeting with BIA commissioner Morris Thompson and Interior Department attorneys shortly after the 1975 occupation began, Edward Cline and other tribal officials resisted the attorneys' efforts to convince them to vacate the land while the government prosecuted a lawsuit on the tribe's behalf. Cline asked, "Why can't we go ahead and make like we own it? We're not going to hassle these people. But we are prepared to defend ourselves." Acknowledging that the BIA should have resolved the matter years earlier, but also believing that violence and bloodshed were imminent, Interior Department solicitor Kent Frizzell begged the Omahas to leave the property and give him a chance to fight their battle in court "with clean hands."[37] Cline reluctantly agreed to discuss Frizzell's recommendations with the full tribal membership, but the Omahas did not move off the property, and even bigger disagreements with the government attorneys loomed.

On May 19, 1975, the U.S. Department of Justice, acting in the capacity of trustee for the Omaha tribe, filed suit in the Federal District Court for the Northern District of Iowa seeking to establish that approximately twenty-nine hundred acres within the original Barrett survey of the Blackbird Bend meander lobe belonged to the Omaha tribe.[38] In its complaint, docketed as Case C75-4024, the government also asked for immediate injunctive relief allowing the tribe to maintain control of the land it had occupied since April 2.

Far from being appeased by this long-awaited action taken by their purported trustee, the Omahas were outraged by the allegations in the government's complaint. The tribe viewed the government's claim as precipitous and unduly "constricted," asserting Omaha title to only a small fraction of the total acreage that the tribe felt it owned. More grievously, the Omahas believed that the Department of Justice attorneys were acting in concert with Iowa state officials and the "politically and financially powerful squatters occupying the Tribe's lands" to defraud the tribe.[39]

Kent Frizzell defended the government's action as a legitimate attempt to forestall violence and bloodshed at Blackbird Bend.[40] In a letter to Cline, Frizzell wrote: "I can appreciate the tribe's justifiable frustration after 40 years of trying to secure department support for its title claim. I cannot be responsible for, nor can I justify, past inaction. By the same token, I cannot rectify the consequences of that action overnight. Courts exist so as to settle controversies in an orderly fashion. The alternative to such settlement is too often bloodshed."[41]

On the day after the government filed its quiet title action in Case 4024, the tribe filed a complaint of its own, prepared by private counsel John T. O'Brien of Sioux City, asking that the Iowa claimants be restrained from interfering with the tribe's possession of the land.[42] That suit, docketed as Case c75-4026, did not seek quiet title to any of the disputed land because the Omahas felt that more preparation was necessary if they were to establish conclusively their ownership of *all* the land at issue. Rather, the tribe sought only to maintain its occupancy of the land and, just as significantly, to serve notice of their strong opposition to the constricted complaint filed on their behalf by the federal government on the previous day.[43]

Two weeks later, the Omahas filed a motion to dismiss the government's complaint in Case 4024, arguing that the tribe's interests were not being adequately represented in that proceeding.[44] In a tribal resolution attached to the motion, the Omahas contended that they had been "grossly and completely abandoned by the Department of Justice" and that the attorney general and the secretary of the interior had breached their trust responsibilities by secretly acting in concert with the Iowa claimants.[45]

The Indians argued that the U.S. attorneys who prepared, filed, and prosecuted the complaint in Case 4024 had limited the tribe's claim to only 2,900 of the total 6,390 acres within the Blackbird Bend lobe and had completely abandoned the tribe's claim to approximately 5,000 additional acres in two areas north of Blackbird Bend known as the Monona Bend and the Omaha Mission Bend tracts.[46] The Omahas' anger was exacerbated by the fact that the U.S. attorney who filed the complaint in Case 4024, Evan L. Hultman, had previously served as attorney general for the state of Iowa. In that capacity, Hultman had represented the state in the earlier quiet title actions among the various Iowa claimants. Those cases had been settled by dividing the Blackbird Bend lobe among the Iowa claimants and the state. As a result, the state of Iowa, formerly represented by the same man who now purported to represent the Omahas, now claimed title to about 700 acres of the land sought by the tribe.

Later events gave the Omahas additional reason to doubt Hultman's devotion to their cause. In the summer of 1976, he served as the lead federal prosecutor in the murder trial of two Indians for the killing of two FBI agents on the Pine Ridge reservation the previous summer. The Indian defendants were acquitted by a Cedar Rapids jury, and some Omahas became convinced that, "Since he [Hultman] couldn't get us [Indians] there, he would be sure to get us at Blackbird Bend."[47] Regardless of whether those doubts were justified, at least one BIA official acknowledged the potential effect of Hultman's role in the reservation murders case on the Blackbird Bend litigation. On August 9, 1976, Martin E. Seneca Jr., director of the BIA's Office of Trust Responsibility, expressed misgivings about allowing Hultman's office to handle the Blackbird Bend case on behalf of the Omahas since "the recent acquittals in the Pine Ridge murder trials have intensified local tensions between Indians and non-Indians."[48] Seneca's concerns were ignored.

On June 5, 1975, federal district judge Edward J. McManus consolidated the two cases for hearing on the requests for injunctive relief and granted the Omahas a preliminary injunction allowing them to continue their occupancy of the land while the litigation was pending. McManus's order also required, however, that all proceeds from the tribe's farming operations on the land be deposited with the court and held in escrow until title to the property could be determined.[49]

Several weeks later, Judge McManus denied the Omahas' motion to dismiss the government's complaint, holding that the tribe's arguments regarding U.S. Attorney Hultman's conflict of interest were "without merit at this time."[50] The Omahas viewed this as simply another example of the government conspiracy against them, inasmuch as McManus had been the lieutenant governor of Iowa at the time of the earlier intrastate litigation regarding the Blackbird Bend lands and was thus well aware of Hultman's prior connection to the case. Over the ensuing years, the federal courts would repeatedly reject the tribe's continuing allegations of fraud and conspiracy among the government attorneys, often imposing sanctions on the tribe for repeatedly raising what the courts deemed to be "frivolous" claims.[51] Nevertheless, the fraud charges would resonate throughout the extended course of the litigation, creating a disturbing atmosphere of hostility that would ultimately contribute to the dismissal of the tribe's claims for most of the land it sought.

By October 1975, the Omahas had completed the preparation of their claim for *all* the Iowa land to which they felt entitled. On October 6, their attorney, John T. O'Brien, filed the tribe's second independent complaint in the Blackbird Bend proceedings. In the new action, docketed as Case c75-4067, the Omahas named nearly a hundred separate Iowa landowners as defendants and asserted title to three separate tracts of land totaling 11,300 acres on the eastern side of the river.[52] Tract 1 encompassed an additional 3,490 acres within the Blackbird Bend meander lobe (in addition to the 2,900 acres within the Barrett survey claimed for the tribe in the government's suit). Tract 2 was the Monona Bend area located north of Blackbird Bend, comprising 4,185 acres. Tract 3 was a 725-acre parcel farther to the north known as Omaha Mission Bend (see map 6). In addition, the tribe's complaint asked for damages in the amount of $50 million for the defendants' wrongful use of the land over the previous fifty years, in contrast to the government's complaint for the Omahas, which sought no monetary relief.

As the dozens of Iowans named in the Omahas' complaint were served with court notices in the case, tensions in the region rose again. Some of the defendants joined forces to fight the lawsuit, creating an organization called the Monona County Landowner's Association, and hiring former Iowa congressman Wiley Mayne as their attorney.[53] All the named defendants expressed a common resolve to fight for the land they had farmed for generations, with Mrs. Howard Miller voicing a common sentiment: "My dad bought this land from the man who homesteaded it. He bought that land, we have title to it and we're not giving it up."[54] Mayne counseled his clients to refrain

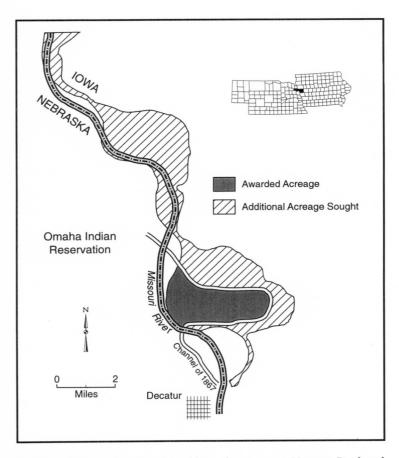

6. **Missouri River,** depicting the additional acreage at Monona Bend and Omaha Mission Bend sought by the Omaha tribe. Courtesy of State Historical Society of Iowa.

from resorting to "self-help" measures in defense of their land, despite their understandable shock and anger at being told that they were not rightfully entitled to their property.[55]

The Omahas responded to the Iowans with equal indignation, publicly asserting that those who were now complaining about the tribe's claim had known for years that the land belonged to the tribe and had been merely "squatting on the land for the last fifty years." Their attorney, John O'Brien, defended his clients to reporters, stating: "A great number of people who live there [in Monona County] took over the land when the Missouri was a wild river. They ran people off it and claimed it for their own when it was really Indian land. . . . You're going to hear they [the Omahas] are no-good, lazy devils. But they're hard working people trying to get ahead like anyone else."[56]

Edward Cline reported that shots had been fired at the Omahas who were occupying the land but that "authorities had failed to take action." Despite those hostilities, Cline expressed sympathy for the Iowans who were going to lose land to the Omahas. He argued, however, that the fault lay, not with the Indians, but rather with the Iowans' attorneys, who had failed to warn them of the potential problems with their title at the time they acquired the land.[57]

On January 26, 1976, Judge McManus granted a motion filed by the Omahas seeking to have the three pending cases consolidated for trial.[58] In so doing, he placed in issue the title to *all* the Iowa land claimed by the Omahas, thereby effectively overriding the government's constricted complaint filed on the Omaha's behalf. Three months later, however, the judge reversed course. On April 5, 1976, he entered a new order in which he held that the tribe's allegations in Case 4067 were "hindering an orderly and efficient administration of justice."[59] McManus therefore severed the Omaha's claims for the additional acreage outside the Barrett survey area in Blackbird Bend and their claims for the lands at Monona Bend and Omaha Mission Bend. The net effect of this crucial April 5 decree was to cause the case to proceed to trial on the constricted complaint originally filed by the government, leaving the Omahas' claims for the much larger additional areas on hold for more than eight years.[60] While it might be argued that the severance order was grounded in legitimate procedural concerns, to the Omahas it signaled a judicial sellout of their claims and offered further evidence of a continuing government conspiracy.[61]

The case proceeded to trial in Sioux City before Judge Andrew W. Bogue on the issue of title to the twenty-nine hundred acres within the Barrett survey.[62] From November 1 to December 6, 1976, the parties presented voluminous and complex expert testimony and scores of maps, charts, and other documentary evidence seeking to establish the precise nature of the movements of the Missouri River from 1867 until the 1940s.[63]

From a purely legal perspective, the dispositive issue before the court became relatively straightforward. Under centuries-old principles of riparian property law, land that is moved to the opposite side of a river by reason of an avulsion remains the property of the original landowner. Courts have traditionally defined an avulsion as the sudden and clearly perceptible shift of identifiable land from one side of a river to the other. If, on the other hand, a river's current causes land on one side of the river gradually to erode away and slowly "re-emerge" by sedimentary action on the opposite side, the newly created land is considered an accretion to the property of the owner on that side of the river.[64] At Blackbird Bend, therefore, the Omahas generally argued that their land had been shifted to the Iowa side by avulsion, while the Iowans claimed that the operative geologic forces had been those of erosion and accretion.[65]

While the relevant legal doctrines could thus be succinctly stated, the application of those principles to the movements of the Missouri River in the Blackbird Bend area from the 1860s to the 1940s was not nearly as clear-cut. A full examination of the massive amounts of evidence offered by the parties relating to the movements of the river is beyond my scope here and is best presented in Judge Bogue's painstakingly detailed analysis contained in his published decisions in the case.[66] The difficulty of the court's task is reflected in *dicta* offered by the judge within his opinion: "The events which the court is obliged to reconstruct occurred long ago and they were events of nature; so far as we know these events were not observed in their entirety by any person who could today be a witness concerning them. . . . it becomes apparent that the movements of the Missouri River have not been so clean and precise that they easily fall into legal categories conveyed by the terms 'accretion' and 'avulsion.'"[67]

Despite those misgivings, Judge Bogue ultimately ruled in favor of the Iowa landowners. He held that the Omahas had failed to sustain their burden of proving that the Blackbird Bend area had been detached from their reservation and redeposited on the Iowa side of the river in a manner consistent with the theory of avulsion. Accordingly, he awarded title to all the disputed land within the Barrett survey to the Iowa defendants and ordered that the funds generated by the Omahas' farming operations during the previous two years be paid to them as well.[68]

The continuing emotional and moral complexity of the dispute was reflected in a supplemental letter from the court delivered to the parties at the time of the decision. In the letter, Judge Bogue took the unusual step of revealing his personal feelings about the equities of the case. He wrote of his "distaste for the laws of avulsion and accretion which have brought about this seemingly unfair result" and criticized the original creators of the reservation for failing to define the boundaries "by degrees of longitude and latitude or some other permanent type of description." Bogue went on to declare that Blackbird Bend "should have remained the property of the Tribe for evermore no matter whether it was under water or divided in whole or in part by water, and no matter how it got that way." He concluded by suggesting that "the least that should be done is for the Congress to reimburse the Tribe for its loss. If this Court had the power to order such payment, you can rest assured it would be done."[69]

The district court's personal sentiments did little to comfort the Omahas. Incensed by the decision, they vowed to remain on the land despite the court's dissolution of the June 5, 1975, injunction that had given the tribe temporary possession. When Monona County sheriff Albert Wood and county attorney Stephen Allen served the occupying Omahas with a court order to vacate the property, Edward Cline told them that the tribe would not comply inasmuch as their attorneys were in the process of appealing the district court's decision.[70] As county officials began to mobilize to remove the Indians by force, the Eighth Circuit Court of Appeals stepped in, issuing a temporary stay of Judge

Bogue's decision.[71] That temporary order was subsequently extended, allowing the tribe to remain in possession of the land indefinitely.[72]

On April 11, 1978, the court of appeals reversed the district court's decision and ordered that title to the land be vested in the Omaha tribe and the United States as trustee.[73] Like Judge Bogue's opinion in the district court, the Eighth Circuit's published decision contains a comprehensive analysis of both the voluminous evidence presented in the trial of the case and the complex principles of law applicable to those facts. Although the appellate court disagreed with certain portions of Judge Bogue's analysis regarding the defining characteristics of avulsion and accretion, the more fundamental basis for its reversal of the trial court's decision was less esoteric.

Writing for a unanimous three-judge panel, Judge Donald Lay held that the district court had improperly placed the burden of proof on the Omahas. Lay cited a rarely invoked federal statute enacted in 1834 that provides: "In all trials about the right of property in which an Indian may be a party on one side, and a white person on the other, *the burden of proof shall rest upon the white person,* whenever the Indian shall make out a presumption of title in himself from the fact of previous possession or ownership" (emphasis added).[74] Judge Lay held that the 1854 treaty established the Omahas' "previous possession and ownership" of the land within the original Barrett survey. Thus, under the statute, the tribe was entitled to a presumption of title in its favor, and the burden of proof fell on the Iowans to establish that the land had been entirely eroded away from the reservation and accreted to the opposite side.[75]

After an exhaustive analysis of the massive trial record, this time in the context of the reallocated burden of proof, the circuit court ultimately held that the Iowa claimants had established "only speculative inferences" as to whether the river channel had moved as a result of accretion or avulsion.[76] Accordingly, the court held that the Iowans had failed to sustain *their* burden of proof at trial, thus necessitating judgment in favor of the Omahas.

Just as Judge Bogue had expressed his personal distaste for the result at the trial court level, the appellate court acknowledged the seemingly harsh effect of its decision: "We recognize that to require [the Iowans] to prove the cause of the river's movement occurring some 100 years after the event is indeed an onerous burden. This may seem to be an injustice when one considers that the [Iowans] have possessed and continuously farmed the land without protest for nearly 40 years. However, . . . the clear policy of the federal government mandates that the interests of the Omaha Indian Tribe be given their historical and statutory protection. These important possessory land interests cannot be taken away on proof that is basically speculative and conjectural."[77]

Naturally, the Omahas were gratified by the court of appeals decision, while the Iowans expressed "shock and disappointment." Thomas Burke, the attorney representing one of the losing claimants, called the decision a "travesty" that would have far-ranging adverse consequences in other Indian land claims across the country.[78] The Iowans asked the U.S. Supreme Court to accept the case for review, arguing that the 1834 statute created an unconstitutional judicial preference for Indians based solely on race.[79]

In November 1978, the Supreme Court agreed to hear the case.[80] As the parties filed their briefs and awaited the Court's decision, strong feelings continued to simmer at Blackbird Bend. Harold Sorenson, one of the Iowa farmers who claimed part of the disputed land, expressed concern about the future stability of land titles throughout the region, predicting, "If [the Omahas] win this one, there's nothing to keep them from just keeping on going." The Omahas likewise viewed the fight in terms of its effect on the future, but for them the essence of the matter was different. As tribal council member Clifford Wolfe Sr. told a reporter: "We think about our children and grandchildren. From the income [derived from the Blackbird Bend land], maybe they'll feel like we're people. Maybe it'll help their schooling, give them something to fall back on. We want that land back. Anyway we can get it back, we want it back."[81]

On June 20, 1979, the Supreme Court rendered its decision.[82] Like so many decisions of the high court, its opinion in the Blackbird Bend case failed to settle the matter outright, instead returning the case to the lower courts for further consideration. The Supreme Court declared that the Eighth Circuit had been correct in its application of the "burden of proof" statute to the individual Iowa claimants but that it had erred in applying the statute against the state of Iowa itself since a state could not be considered a "white person" under the terms of the statute.

On remand, the circuit court reconsidered its analysis of the issues but once again decided the case largely in favor of the Omahas.[83] The court entered a final judgment awarding all but seven hundred of the twenty-nine hundred acres within the Barrett survey area to the tribe. As to the seven hundred acres claimed by the state of Iowa, the court returned the case once again to the district court for further consideration, with instructions to place the burden of proof back on the tribe.

Over the next eleven years, the seemingly interminable litigation bounced back and forth between the district court and the Eighth Circuit Court of Appeals five more times on the issue of title to the seven hundred acres claimed by the state.[84] As the courts continued to reject the Omahas' claims of conspiracy and fraud, relations between the tribe and the federal district court deteriorated beyond repair. When Judge McManus issued an order in the spring of 1987 awarding the remaining land in dispute to the state, members of the tribe physically barred surveyors from the land. McManus held the entire tribal council in contempt of court and jailed them overnight. They were released only after a tribal resolution was passed agreeing to abide by the court's orders. The adoption of the resolution became a point of substantial internal debate and controversy within the tribe.[85] At a hearing on May 2, 1987, tribal chairman Doran Morris Sr. advised Judge McManus in open court to "go to hell," for which he was promptly jailed again.[86] Later that month, when the judge entered his final judgment and decree in the case, Morris publicly declared that the ruling "proves that he's a racist."[87]

Ultimately, the courts held that the Omahas had failed to meet their burden of proving title to the remaining seven hundred acres in dispute and awarded the land to the state of Iowa. Approximately three hundred additional acres were awarded to various other non-Indian claimants for parcels that had previously been acquired by "fee patents." Thus, when the "Blackbird Bend I" litigation finally ground to a halt sixteen years after it commenced, the Omahas had been awarded title to approximately nineteen hundred of the twenty-nine hundred acres within the Barrett survey. In addition, the erstwhile owners of the land were awarded a judgment against the United States for almost $2 million, plus prejudgment interest, for the value of the improvements made to the property before it was returned to the tribe.

Meanwhile, the tribe's claims to the acreage outside the Barrett survey within the Blackbird Bend lobe and to the additional land in the Monona Bend and Omaha Mission Bend areas to the north remained to be resolved (see map 6 above). Those much larger claims, which now became known as "Blackbird Bend II," had been severed and placed in abeyance by Judge McManus in 1979. As the claims in Blackbird Bend I were resolved, Blackbird Bend II took center stage.[88]

The dozens of Iowa farmers whose lands were at issue in Blackbird Bend II had been following the convoluted proceedings in Blackbird Bend I for years. As the threat to their lands was resurrected, tension within the community rose to new heights. Monona County sheriff Albert Wood bluntly predicted bloodshed if the Omahas sought to "occupy" any of the contested land: "The boys have deeds to the land. They have paid taxes on it. They aren't about to give it up. If they get pushed too hard, I know what will happen. The river will run red."[89]

Although Wood's dire prediction of violence proved to be overstated, the Omahas' attempts to proceed with their remaining claims ultimately deteriorated into a long series of acrimonious confrontations and ad hominem attacks between the tribe's counsel, the attorneys for the Iowa landowners, and the federal judiciary. The evolution of the Omahas private legal representation was, like all other aspects of the litigation, complex and convoluted. After he filed the Omahas' independent action in October 1975, the tribe's original counsel, John T. O'Brien, was supplanted as counsel of record by his brother, Donald E. O'Brien, a former county prosecutor. Their fees were paid by the Department of the Interior, which later assigned one of its staff attorneys, William H. Veeder, to assist in the case. Veeder and Donald O'Brien tried the case on behalf of the tribe. O'Brien was later appointed to the federal bench himself, and representation of the tribe thereafter rested with Veeder alone. Veeder continued to represent the tribe as private counsel even after he left government service.[90] In

1982, Secretary of the Interior James Watt cut off further funding of the Omahas' continuing appeals—yet another example, in the Omahas' view, of the government conspiracy against them.[91] Nebraska congressman Doug Bereuter agreed with the tribe, telling a news reporter at the time, "I'm upset by the fact that we've had political interference in the lawsuit. It seems to me that the secretary is not meeting his trust responsibility to the tribe."[92]

As the Omahas continued to press their charges of fraud, conflict of interest, and collusion on the part of their opponents and the courts, procedural conflicts and animosity among the attorneys escalated to the point that the district court ultimately imposed the harshest possible sanction against the tribe. On May 29, 1990, federal district judge Warren Urbom entered an order in which he condemned the tribe's attorney, William H. Veeder, for his "systematic pattern of failure to comply with court rules and orders" and *dismissed* all the Omahas' remaining claims.[93] One year later, the Eighth Circuit Court of Appeals upheld Urbom's ruling and assessed a penalty against the tribe of double the costs of the appeal for its continued prosecution of the "frivolous" claims of fraud and conspiracy. The judicial denunciation of William Veeder continued as the court declared: "Mr. Veeder continues to exercise scurrilous disrespect for the judges involved in this case. He stands obsessed with the charges of fraud by Judges McManus and Urbom . . . notwithstanding this court's prior dismissal of such a claim. . . . Mr. Veeder through his continued contumacious refusal to comply with the district court orders has done a great disservice to his client in important litigation. It is unfortunate in a case such as this that the client must live or die by the conduct of its counsel."[94] When the Supreme Court denied the tribe's request that it review the case later that year, the Omahas' claims were finally extinguished. Four more years would pass, however, before the courts resolved the last remaining issue in the case.

After the dismissal of the Omahas' claims in Blackbird Bend II became final, two counterclaims against the tribe remained viable. Those counterclaims had been filed by the Iowans whose land the tribe had physically occupied since 1975, and they remained at issue because the tribe continued to occupy the property even after the dismissal of all its remaining claims. In April 1993, the district court gave title to the land to the Iowans and awarded them more than $400,000 for the rental value of the land during the tribe's occupancy. In January 1995, the Eighth Circuit affirmed the district court's decision, and the twenty-nine-year-old legal struggle for Blackbird Bend finally came to an end.[95]

While the Iowans expressed joy and relief at the final disposition of the case, the Omahas vowed to fight on, suggesting that they might reoccupy the land or even take their claims to some other forum, such as the United Nations or the World Court.[96] No such action was ever taken, although the tribe did make a futile request to the Senate Judiciary Committee for an oversight hearing to investigate its grievances against the judges and government attorneys.[97] Notwithstanding the Omahas' lingering discontent, their legal claims to the rest of the disputed land have been permanently extinguished. The tribe has been left with the nineteen hundred acres awarded to it in the Blackbird Bend I litigation, and the Iowans whose land had been threatened in Blackbird Bend II have escaped on procedural grounds, without being required to defend the Omahas' claims on the merits.

A complete epilogue to the Blackbird Bend story remains to be written. It is too soon to draw any sweeping conclusions about the long-term effect of the litigation on the Omahas or their neighbors. Nevertheless, several summative observations can be made. First and foremost, the struggle for Blackbird Bend provides a compelling example of the vexing uncertainties and inherent contradictions that pervade the federal government's trust relationship with Native American tribes. If debacles like the government's forced representation of the Omahas at Blackbird Bend are to be avoided in the future, the precise nature and extent of those trust responsibilities must be reexamined and more clearly delineated. Mechanisms must be instituted to resolve adversarial conflicts between the trustee and the beneficiary *before* the rights of the ward are foreclosed as they were at Blackbird Bend.[98]

As previously noted, another tangible legacy of the litigation may be found in the residue of resentment and frustration that lingers in and around Monona County today. While almost all the local landowners who were named in the litigation ultimately retained title to their land, the years of uncertainty and substantial legal expense that they incurred have left their mark. Vincent Willey, the original chairman of the Monona County Landowners Association, provides a useful description of the local sentiment: "I've got empathy for many of the tribe's people, but things definitely got kind of hot there for a while. The lawsuits tied up everyone's land, held up estates, and generally created tremendous chaos. The people who stayed in the case to the end wound up spending between $150 and $160 per acre to defend their title to land that they held patents on for decades. There definitely is still some resentment."[99]

One of the great ironies of the Blackbird Bend story is the fact that the Omahas share their opponents' sense of lingering frustration. Wynema Morris, a member of the tribal council during much of the litigation, acknowledges a lasting "bitter resentment" at the way in which the courts ultimately derailed the tribe's claim for the vast majority of the land they still feel is theirs: "My mother still looks to that land and has a real visceral feel that it is our land. She gets very emotional whenever we get near Blackbird Bend. We know it is our land—the land of our ancestors. We still want it back. After all, our ancestors are the dust beneath our feet."[100] The Blackbird Bend litigation also contributed to a continuing pattern of dissension and factionalism within the tribe itself, as tribal members debated, sometimes quite vehemently, decisions that were made throughout the long process.[101]

On a more positive note, it may certainly be said that the struggle for Blackbird Bend represents one of the most significant steps taken by the Omaha tribe in the last few decades to resurrect itself as a vibrant and economically viable political and cultural entity. The courts' dismissal of most of the Omahas' claims as a punitive measure against the tribe's attorney casts an unsettling cloud on that determined effort. Nevertheless, the Omahas take a measure of satisfaction in the fact that a portion of the land that they recovered in Iowa is now the site of the tribe's successful gaming operation, CasinOmaha. That enterprise, combined with the farming operations on the remainder of the land, has contributed significantly to the tribal revenue base over the past several years. They provide the most tangible positive legacy of the Omahas' "imperfect victory" at Blackbird Bend.

4. CasinOmaha at Blackbird Bend, October 1995. Photo by the author.

5. Omaha tribal farming operations at Blackbird Bend, October 1995. Photo by the author.

Conclusion

Throughout its long history, the Omaha tribe has exhibited a cultural resiliency that is both remarkable and inspiring. In the eighteenth and nineteenth centuries, the Omahas weathered literally every challenge that federal and state policymakers could place before them, from the repeated violations of solemn treaties to the disastrous allotment of tribal lands.[1] In the modern era as well, the Omahas' resolve to maintain their political and cultural viability has been repeatedly put to the test—in the lawlessness of the PL 280 years, the quest for retrocession, the long and tedious journey through the Indian Claims Commission, and the even more protracted odyssey of the Blackbird Bend litigation.

To a significant extent, the Omahas have emerged from these struggles as a stronger and more resolute political and cultural entity. By aggressively pursuing, and ultimately achieving, these "imperfect victories"—in the halls of Congress, the state legislature, the Indian Claims Commission, and the federal courts—the tribe has achieved a significant measure of compensation for centuries of past abuse. With the establishment of a tribal law enforcement structure through retrocession, the creation of numerous economic development projects with the proceeds of the ICC judgments, and the opening of CasinOmaha and additional tribal farming operations on the Iowa land regained in the Blackbird Bend litigation, the Omahas have made substantial strides toward a more secure future. During the last few years, a sense of restrained optimism on the reservation has replaced more than one hundred years of deprivation and despair.[2] As tribal member Wayne Tyndall recently observed, "People are working more than ever before. There is more self-esteem, and people are becoming more self-suffi-

115

cient. The casino has really changed the complexion of the overall community. Everyone is thankful for that."[3]

Certainly, CasinOmaha has been the key to much of the recent improvement in the reservation economy and morale. As profits from the casino replenish the tribal treasury, Omaha leaders are striving to invest those proceeds in ways that will produce the best possible long-term return. Just as with the ICC judgments, the tribe has distributed a portion of the annual casino profits to its members on a per capita basis.[4] The remainder of the annual revenues has been used for a multitude of development programs, including road repairs, school renovation and supplies, scholarship programs, the expansion of health facilities, water system improvements, and a youth emergency shelter. The tribe is working with government officials and independent consultants to develop and implement a comprehensive plan designed to bring sorely needed commercial enterprise to the once-impoverished reservation.[5]

Yet much remains to be done. As both tribal leaders and outside observers have acknowledged, the revenues generated by CasinOmaha are not a panacea for all the tribe's remaining concerns. The tribe is acutely aware that the gambling well may run dry at any time.[6] Indeed, as competing casinos take root in Council Bluffs, Iowa, and elsewhere, and as Indian gaming operations throughout the country draw increasing congressional scrutiny, the future of the Omahas' relatively isolated casino is far from certain.

As the Omahas look to the future, chronic problems linger for tribal attention. Among many other issues, the tribe must address pressing concerns related to drug and alcohol abuse, educational and medical deficiencies, and a continuing internal factionalism between on- and off-reservation members. Like all other tribes across the country, the Omahas must also prepare to weather impending reductions in federal funding for Indian services.[7] These and many other serious concerns cry out for additional academic exploration and, more important, strong remedial action.

Whatever problems remain to be addressed, however, the members of the Omaha tribe can and should take strength from the remarkable perseverance demonstrated by their forebears. As this book is designed to demonstrate, the Omahas' collective character as survivors has been as notable in the modern era as at any other time in the tribe's long history. By withstanding the "dragon's nest" of PL 280, forging ahead with retrocession, and enduring years of litigation in the ICC and the federal courts, the Omahas have created for themselves an enduring foundation of political and cultural tenacity. That legacy should serve them well as they confront the challenges of the twenty-first century.

Notes

Introduction

1. Fortunately, the early history of the Omaha tribe has been the subject of two recent, exemplary works, both of which have been consulted thoroughly in preparing this brief synthesis. David J. Wishart's *An Unspeakable Sadness: The Dispossession of the Nebraska Indians* (Lincoln: University of Nebraska Press, 1997) traces the history of all the Nebraska Indian tribes from the late eighteenth through the twentieth centuries, with abundant detail and insight into the Omahas' story. Judith A. Boughter's *Betraying the Omaha Nation, 1790–1916* (Norman: University of Oklahoma Press, 1998) is focused exclusively on the Omahas, providing a remarkably comprehensive examination of the tribe's origins and evolution, with particular emphasis on nineteenth- and early twentieth-century developments. See also Robin Ridington, "Omaha Survival: A Vanishing Indian Tribe That Would Not Vanish," *American Indian Quarterly* 11 (winter 1987): 37–51.

2. Alice C. Fletcher and Francis La Flesche, *The Omaha Tribe* (Lincoln: University of Nebraska Press, 1972), 1:70–71.

3. Boughter, *Betraying the Omaha Nation,* chap. 1.

4. Wishart, *An Unspeakable Sadness,* 23–25. Boughter, *Betraying Their Trust,* chap. 1.

5. Wishart, *An Unspeakable Sadness,* 18.

6. Robin Ridington and Dennis Hastings, *Blessing for a Long Time: The Sacred Pole of the Omaha Tribe* (Lincoln: University of Nebraska Press, 1997).

7. Boughter, *Betraying the Omaha Nation,* chap. 1.

8. Wishart, *An Unspeakable Sadness,* 7.

9. Boughter, *Betraying the Omaha Nation,* chap. 1.

10. Wishart, *An Unspeakable Sadness*, 153.

11. Wishart, *An Unspeakable Sadness*, 154.

12. Wishart, *An Unspeakable Sadness*, 235.

13. Wishart, *An Unspeakable Sadness*, 238.

14. Michael L. Tate, *The Upstream People: An Annotated Research Bibliography of the Omaha Tribe* (Metuchen NJ: Scarecrow, 1991), vii.

1. Arrival of PL 280

1. *U.S. Statutes at Large* 67 (August 1, 1953): B132.

2. It has been accurately noted that "practically every commentary on Public Law 280 begins with a sentence or paragraph which refers to the pendulum swing in federal policy between Indian 'self-determination' and Indian 'termination'" (*Final Report to the American Indian Policy Review Commission, Task Force Four: Federal, State, and Tribal Jurisdiction* [Washington DC: U.S. Government Printing Office, 1976], 4). This book obviously follows the same pattern, but it will not expand that discussion other than to note that general treatments of federal Indian policy are available in numerous sources, including Rennard Strickland and Charles F. Wilkinson, eds., *Felix S. Cohen's Handbook of Federal Indian Law*, rev. ed. (Charlottesville VA: Michie Bobbs-Merrill, 1982); John R. Wunder, *"Retained by the People": A History of American Indians and the Bill of Rights* (New York: Oxford University Press, 1994); William C. Canby Jr., *American Indian Law*, Nutshell Series (St. Paul MN: West, 1988), 9–31; and *Justice and the American Indian: The Impact of Public Law 280 upon the Administration of Justice on Indian Reservations* (Washington DC: National American Indian Court Judges Association, 1974), chap. 1, "A Short History of Federal Policy Vacillation toward Indians," 18–34.

3. Wunder, *"Retained by the People,"* 48–49.

4. Lewis Meriam and Henry Roe Cloud, *The Problem of Indian Administration* (Baltimore: Johns Hopkins University Press, 1928).

5. For a full account of the Meriam Report, see Wunder, *"Retained by the People,"* 54–58, and the sources cited therein.

6. Wunder, *"Retained by the People,"* 72.

7. For an overview of Indian opposition to Collier's programs, see Wunder, *"Retained by the People,"* 66–71, and the sources cited therein. See also Lau-

rence M. Hauptman, "The Indian Reorganization Act," in *The Aggressions of Civilization*, ed. Sandra A. Cadwalader and Vine Deloria Jr. (Philadelphia: Temple University Press, 1984), who observes that recent assessments of Collier's reign have been increasingly critical. For a more favorable assessment of Collier's tenure as commissioner of Indian affairs, see Kenneth R. Philp, *John Collier's Crusade for Indian Reform, 1920–1954* (Tucson: University of Arizona Press, 1977).

8. Wunder, *"Retained by the People,"* 66.

9. For more on the Hoover Commission Report, see Vine Deloria Jr. and Clifford M. Lytle, *American Indians, American Justice* (Austin: University of Texas Press, 1983), 16–17; and Donald L. Fixico, *Termination and Relocation: Federal Indian Policy, 1945–1960* (Albuquerque: University of New Mexico Press, 1986), 45–62.

10. A particularly useful overview of the origins and evolution of the termination movement may be found in Charles F. Wilkinson and Eric R. Biggs, "The Evolution of the Termination Policy," *American Indian Law Review* 5, no. 1 (1977): 139–84.

11. For strident criticism of Myer's public career, see Richard Drinnon, *Keeper of Concentration Camps: Dillon S. Myer and American Racism* (Berkeley: University of California Press, 1987).

12. Dillon S. Myer to All Tribal Council Members, October 10, 1952, box 2, file "Government Agencies," folder 1, Dillon S. Myer Papers, Harry S. Truman Presidential Library, Independence MO. (References to documents in this collection will hereafter be cited as Myer Papers, with box and folder designations as appropriate.)

13. For example, in a speech presented to the Western Governor's Conference in Phoenix AZ on December 9, 1952, Myer stated, "While I am encouraged by the progress that has been made to date in the transfer of service responsibilities, I believe strongly that we have not moved far enough or fast enough in this direction. During the past two years we have been placing increased emphasis on speeding up progress toward these objectives" (Myer Papers, box 2, folder 1).

14. U.S. Senate, Senator Butler speaking on removal of restrictions on certain Indian tribes, 80th Cong., 2d sess., *Congressional Record* (July 21, 1947), 93:9465.

15. U.S. Senate, Senator Butler speaking on "Are Indians Wards of the Government?" 81st Cong., 2d sess., *Congressional Record* (March 29, 1950), 96:A2368.

16. U.S. Senate, Senator Butler speaking on Malone bill to abolish Bureau of Indian Affairs, 81st Cong., 2d sess., *Congressional Record* (October 16, 1951), 96:A6433.

17. Arthur V. Watkins, "Termination of Federal Supervision: The Removal of Restrictions over Indian Property and Person," *Annals of the American Academy of Political and Social Science* 311 (May 1957): 55.

18. U.S. House, Representative William H. Harrison speaking in support of House Concurrent Resolution 108, 83d Cong., 1st sess., *Congressional Record* (July 20, 1953), 99:9363.

19. Frank George, Executive Director, National Congress of American Indians, to All Tribal Council Chairmen, September 26, 1952, Myer Papers, box 2, folder 1.

20. Resolution on Indian Affairs, adopted by the Biennial Convention of the National Farmers Union, March 1954, box 77, file "Association on American Indians, Correspondence 1953–54," Philleo Nash Papers, Harry S. Truman Presidential Library, Independence MO.

21. Dorothy Bohn, "'Liberating' the Indian, Euphemism for a Land Grab," *The Nation* 178 (February 10, 1954): 150–51.

22. John Collier, "Back to Dishonor," *Christian Century* 71 (May 12, 1954): 578–80.

23. John Collier, Press Release, December 15, 1952, Myer Papers, box 2, folder 3. The animosity between Collier and Myer was personal and chronic, dating back to at least 1942 (see Philp, *John Collier's Crusade*, 225–28).

24. Sandra A. Cadwalader and Vine Deloria Jr., introduction to *The Aggressions of Civilization*, xiv. For additional analysis of the impetus for termination, see Fixico, *Termination and Relocation*, 111–13.

25. Dillon S. Myer, Memorandum to Secretary of the Interior, March 20, 1953, Myer Papers, folder 2.

26. The effects of termination on the Northern Ponca are lamented with particular poignancy in the words of an anonymous tribal member quoted in Wunder, *"Retained by the People,"* 172–73.

27. Comprehensive discussions of these cases include Stephen Herzberg, "The Menominee Indians: Termination to Restoration," *American Indian Law Review* 6, no. 1 (1978): 143–86; and Susan Hood, "Termination of the Klamath Tribe of Oregon," *Ethnohistory* 19 (fall 1972): 372–92. By the early 1960s, the termination policy was almost universally recognized as a failure.

28. Wunder, *"Retained by the People,"* 102.

29. *U.S. Statutes at Large* 67 (August 15, 1953): 588.

30. The original mandatory states, in addition to Nebraska, were California, Minnesota, Oregon, and Wisconsin. The law was amended in 1958 to include Alaska as well. The criminal jurisdiction provisions of PL 280 are codified at 18 U.S.C. sec. 1162 (1953), while civil jurisdiction is codified at 28 U.S.C. sec. 1360 (1953).

31. Under sec. 6 of the act, "disclaimer optional states" were those that had been expressly required to disclaim jurisdiction over Indian reservations in their constitutions—Arizona, Montana, New Mexico, North Dakota, Oklahoma, South Dakota, Utah, and Washington. Under sec. 7, "nondisclaimer optional states" were those with no such existing constitutional prohibition. They were empowered to assume Indian jurisdiction simply by appropriate legislation (U.S. Senate, *United States Code Congressional and Administrative News*, 83d Cong., 1st sess., 1953, S. Rept. 699, 2:2409, 2412 [hereafter S. Rept. 699]). These provisions were inserted into the bill at the specific insistence of Nebraska Senator Hugh Butler (see Larry W. Burt, *Tribalism in Crisis: Federal Indian Policy, 1953–1961* [Albuquerque: University of New Mexico Press, 1982], 25; and also Wunder, *"Retained by the People,"* 108).

32. The most thorough treatment of the passage and operation of PL 280 remains Carole E. Goldberg, "Public Law 280: State Jurisdiction over Reservation Indians," *UCLA Law Review* 22 (February 1975): 535–94.

33. S. Rept. 699, 2:2409, 2411.

34. U.S. House Subcommittee on Indian Affairs, Statement of Representative Wesley A. D'Ewert, in *Hearings on H.R. 459, H.R. 3235, and H.R. 3624 before the Subcommittee on Indian Affairs of the Interior and Insular Affairs Comm.*, ser. 11, 82d Cong., 2d sess., February 28, 1952, 16. (These hearings will hereafter be cited as *1952 Hearings*.)

35. Dwight D. Eisenhower, Statement upon Signing of Public Law 280, August 15, 1953, reprinted in *Congressional Record* (January 12, 1956), 102:399.

36. *New York Times*, August 12, 1953, 30.

37. John Collier to Milton Eisenhower, August 6, 1953, quoted in Philp, *John Collier's Crusade*, 229.

38. Collier, "Back to Dishonor," 579. Eisenhower's call for amendments to the act went unheeded, as Collier expected. Seven attempts were made during the Eisenhower administration to rectify this "unfortunate omission," but all

failed passage (Fixico, *Termination and Relocation*, 112). Ultimately, consent requirements were incorporated in the provisions of the Indian Bill of Rights in 1968, but by that time PL 280 was all but dead anyway.

39. U.S. House, 83d Cong., 1st sess., July 16, 1953, H. Rept. 848.

40. U.S. House, 83d Cong., 1st sess., July 16, 1953, H. Rept. 848.

41. Statement of Commissioner of Indian Affairs Dillon S. Myer, *1952 Hearings*, 25, 26.

42. Minutes of the Meeting of Agency Superintendents and Area Personnel with the Commissioner of Indian Affairs, August 29, 1952, Sherman Hotel, Aberdeen SD, Records of the BIA, Winnebago Agency, Record Group 075, box 349 (92M0007), file "Programs, Jurisdiction 1949–52," National Archives—Central Plains Region, Kansas City MO. (References to documents in these records will hereafter be cited as Winnebago Agency Records, National Archives, with box and file designations as appropriate.)

43. Program and Proceedings, Third Annual Conference on Indian Affairs, "Indian Problems of Law and Order," Institute of Indian Studies, State University of South Dakota, June 16–17, 1957, 74.

44. H. E. Bruce to Frank Beaver, Amos Lamson, David Frazier, and Joseph LeRoy, February 23, 1951, Winnebago Agency Records, National Archives, file "Programs, Jurisdiction 1949–52."

45. Resolution of Omaha, Santee Sioux, and Winnebago Tribes, March 9, 1951, Winnebago Agency Records, National Archives, file "Programs, Jurisdiction 1949–52."

46. H. E. Bruce to John R. Nichols, Commissioner of Indian Affairs, May 16, 1949, 51, Winnebago Agency Records, National Archives, file "Programs, Jurisdiction 1949–52."

47. H. E. Bruce to Aberdeen Area Director, March 1, 1951, 2, Winnebago Agency Records, National Archives, file "Programs, Jurisdiction 1949–52."

48. U.S. House, 82d Cong., 2d sess., July 1, 1952, H.R. 698.

49. U.S. House, *Report with Respect to the House Resolution Authorizing the Committee on Interior and Insular Affairs to Conduct an Investigation of the Bureau of Indian Affairs*, 82d Cong, 2d sess., 1953, H. Rept. 2503, table XII, pp. 104–9.

50. *Robinson v Sigler*, 187 Neb. 144, 187 N.W.2d 756 (1971), *Brief of Petitioner and Appellant*, 22. The court rejected this and other constitutional arguments raised by the appellant and upheld the jurisdiction of the state courts under PL 280.

51. Program and Proceedings, "Indian Problems of Law and Order," 76–77.

52. See "Indian Affairs Bureau Informs Nebraska It Has Responsibility," *Lincoln Star,* September 20, 1956, 20.

53. "Indian Affairs Bills Leave Officials Uncertain of Effect," *Lincoln Sunday Journal and Star,* August 9, 1953, 2-A.

54. The *Omaha World-Herald,* the *Walthill Citizen,* and the *Pender Times,* among others, have been examined for the period from 1950 to 1953. None appear to have addressed the issue of PL 280 prior to its passage, although articles discussing jurisdictional problems did begin to appear on a sporadic basis in the years following enactment of the law.

55. PL 280 vested jurisdiction in the state for even those crimes that had previously been specifically reserved to the federal government pursuant to the 1885 Federal Major Crimes Act (*U.S. Statutes at Large* 23 [March 3, 1885]: 385). The seven "major crimes" were murder, manslaughter, rape, assault with intent to kill, arson, burglary, and larceny. Jurisdiction over crimes not so designated was ostensibly vested in the tribes themselves. (The statute was subsequently amended in 1932, and again in 1968, so as ultimately to include kidnapping, statutory rape, assault with intent to rape, incest, assault with a dangerous weapon, and assault resulting in serious bodily harm; see 18 U.S.C. sec. 1153 [1982].) In Nebraska, however, the state courts had stepped in and exercised jurisdiction over all "nonmajor" crimes, for reasons discussed herein.

56. *Robinson v Sigler,* 187 Neb. 144, 187 N.W.2d 756 (1971).

57. The prosecution of Robinson in state court for the crime of murder illustrates the way in which PL 280 superseded the Federal Major Crimes Act in the mandatory states. Prior to 1953, jurisdiction over murder cases involving Indians would have clearly remained in the federal courts.

58. The allotment statute relied on by the state is found at *U.S. Statutes at Large* 22 (August 7, 1882): 341.

59. *U.S. Statutes at Large* 22 (August 7, 1882): 341.

60. *Robinson v Sigler,* 187 Neb. 144, 148, 187 N.W.2d 756, 759.

61. *Robinson v Sigler,* 187 Neb. 144, 148, 187 N.W.2d 756 (1971) *Brief of Appellee,* 11.

62. Senate Subcommittee on Indian Affairs, *Hearings before the Subcommittee on Indian Affairs of the Committee on Interior and Insular Affairs, United States Senate, on S. 2010,* 94th Cong., 2d sess., March 4–5, 1975, pt. 2, p. 471. (These

hearings were conducted in two sessions, the first in December 1975, the second in March 1976. The transcripts, contained in two volumes, offer a wealth of testimony and evidence regarding the Nebraska situation. They will be cited hereafter as *1975–76 Hearings*.)

63. *1975–76 Hearings*, 648, 655–56.

64. *Omaha Tribe of Nebraska v Village of Walthill*, 334 F. Supp. 823, 837 (D. Neb. 1971).

65. Such an examination is, however, available is other sources—see, e.g., Robert N. Clinton, "Criminal Jurisdiction over Indian Lands: A Journey through a Jurisdictional Maze," *Arizona Law Review* 18 (1976): 503, and "Development of Criminal Jurisdiction over Indian Lands: The Historical Perspective," *Arizona Law Review* 17 (1975): 951.

66. Clinton, "The Historical Perspective," 991.

67. For an extended discussion of these issues, see Clinton, "The Historical Perspective," 965–69.

68. *Decisions of the Department of Interior*, M-36184 (February 15, 1954), 61 I.D. 298, 304.

69. *Kitto v State*, 98 Neb. 164, 167, 172 (1915).

70. Nebraska Legislative Council, *Report of the Legislative Council Interim Study Committee on Judiciary-Indian Retrocession*, Committee Report no. 226 (January 1976), vol. 3 (hereafter cited as *1976 Legislative Council Report*).

71. Published decisions from the pre-1953 era in which the Nebraska courts exercised jurisdiction over Indians on the reservations include *Kitto v State*, 98 Neb. 164, 152 N.W. 380 (1915); *Marion v State*, 16 Neb. 349, 20 N.W. 289 (1884); and *Painter v Ives*, 4 Neb. 122 (1875). As noted previously, of course, the state and county courts were also routinely prosecuting Indians in hundreds of unpublished proceedings.

72. An argument could be made, of course, that Nebraska was made a mandatory PL 280 state in order to legitimize or cover up the state's erroneous exercise of jurisdiction. The best that can be said of such a theory is that there appears to be no overt evidence of such an intent in the legislative record.

73. Charles Vollan, a doctoral candidate in history at the University of Nebraska–Lincoln, has conducted extensive analysis of court records in Thurston County for the period of the late 1940s and early 1950s. His research, compiled in a yet-to-be published manuscript, reflects the fact that law-and-order

statistics are exceedingly difficult to track during this period and that it is today virtually impossible to distinguish between Indian and non-Indian cases.

74. Bruce to Nichols, May 16, 1949, 17.

75. Bruce to Nichols, May 16, 1949, 26. Bruce's choice of words is noteworthy here. He assumes Indian guilt in the "commission" of these offenses and does not consider the possibility of selective prosecution on the part of county officials. His numbers nevertheless offer the best available indication of pre-1953 conditions on the reservation.

76. Bruce to Nichols, May 16, 1949, 29. Former Thurston County attorney Al Raun echoed Bruce's comments in 1953, lamenting the county's "unjust load." He stated that, of three hundred criminal cases handled in the county's courts in 1952, about 90 percent had involved Indians ("Indian Law Enforcing Load Heavy, Thurston Co. Bearing Burden," *Lincoln Sunday Journal and Star,* August 30, 1953, 5-A).

77. Bruce to Nichols, May 16, 1949, 41.

2. PL 280 in Operation

1. See n. 55, chap. 1, above.

2. Bruce to Nichols, May 16, 1949, 51.

3. For example, in 1961, Thurston County Board member William Hoppner testified to the Nebraska Legislature that only one federal officer had served on the reservation prior to the transfer of jurisdiction (see "LB 713, Hearing before Government & Military Affairs Committee, May 18, 1961, as Reported by Marvel A. Mitchell, Shorthand Reporter," 12, Winnebago Agency Records, National Archives, box 103, file "Law and Order, 1961–1969" [hereafter cited as "LB 713 Hearing"]; a summary of the hearing may also be found in Betty Person, "Stronger Law Enforcement Is Asked for Reservations," *Lincoln Star,* May 19, 1961, 1). As will be seen below, the transcript of the LB 713 hearing includes testimony from state and local officials as well as both white and Indian residents of Thurston County and provides a wealth of insight into the law enforcement conditions on the reservation during the early years of PL 280 jurisdiction.

4. For example, in 1976, the Nebraska Legislative Council prepared a report in which it summarized the history of PL 280 and Indian jurisdiction in the state. The report seems to imply a larger federal law enforcement presence than ac-

tually existed, stating, "With the transfer of jurisdiction [to the state under PL 280], the Bureau of Indian Affairs immediately withdrew all their law enforcement personnel" (*1976 Legislative Council Report*, 9).

5. "LB 713 Hearing," 6.

6. Robert Agee, "Crimes on Indian Reservation Up," *Omaha World-Herald*, July 10, 1956, 4.

7. Frank Santiago, "Indian, White Chasm Widens," *Omaha World-Herald*, November 1, 1970, 16-B.

8. Quoted in Burt, *Tribalism in Crisis*, 77. See also Wunder, *"Retained by the People,"* 109.

9. Program and Proceedings, "Indian Problems of Law and Order," 77.

10. "State Responsible for Enforcing Law Says Bureau of Indian Affairs," *Walthill Citizen*, September 27, 1956, 3. See also "Sheriff Hopes for Financial Assistance," *Lincoln Star*, August 21, 1956, 9; "Several Northern Counties Facing Indian Problems," *Lincoln Star*, August 22, 1956, 16; and "'Indian Problem Not Jurisdiction,' C. S. Beck Says," *Lincoln Star*, September 21, 1956, 23, where Beck defended the 1951 letter in which he offered the state's "consent" to the passage of PL 280. Beck stated, "No one could object to such a law for a good many reasons, but the main reason is that the state of Nebraska has exercised such jurisdiction since at least 1875."

11. "Message from Gov. Victor E. Anderson to the President, the Speaker, and Members of the Legislature," April 8, 1957, *Nebraska Legislative Journal*, 1957, 1096–97.

12. "Message from Gov. Victor E. Anderson," 1096.

13. Legislative Bill 600, *Laws of Nebraska*, 1957, 293–94. The bill is codified at Nebraska Revised Statutes sec. 23-362 (1957).

14. In October 1957, the state paid Thurston County $243.75 pursuant to the new legislation ("State Pays $243 on Thurston Cost of Feeding Indians," *Lincoln Star*, November 6, 1957, 12).

15. "LB 713 Hearing," 3.

16. "LB 713 Hearing," 6.

17. The question of the Omahas' payment of taxes on their allotted and trust lands has long been a point of confusion and misstatement in Thurston County. The definitive analysis of this issue may be found in Richmond L. Clow, "Taxing the Omaha and Winnebago Trust Lands, 1910–1971: An In-

fringement of the Tax-Immune Status of Indian Country," *American Indian Culture and Research Journal* 9, no. 4 (1985): 1–22. Clow shows that, despite the supposed immunity of tribal lands from state taxes, the Omahas did in fact pay taxes on their trust allotments from 1910 until 1971, just as tribal leaders claimed throughout the PL 280 years.

18. "LB 713 Hearing," 7.

19. "LB 713 Hearing," 8 (Cline), 11 (Ten Haken).

20. *1976 Legislative Council Report*, 9. This report stated that, in the light of the controversy created by LB 713, "Shortly thereafter, it was repealed." That assertion does not appear to be correct. Examination of the legislative history of this statute reveals that it was not amended again until 1967, and even then the amendments did not alter the 60 percent rule (see Legislative Bill 9, *Laws of Nebraska*, 1967, 397–98). This notion that the 60 percent rule was repealed shortly after its passage is also refuted by "Law and Indians Discussion Slated," *Lincoln Star*, August 18, 1972, 1, where it is reported that the Legislature's Judiciary Committee had decided to seek the repeal of the "Indian Bounty Act" *during the 1973 session*. The repeal finally occurred on April 12, 1974, via Legislative Bill 131, *Laws of Nebraska*, 1974, 68–69.

21. *1976 Legislative Council Report*.

22. Agee, "Crimes on Indian Reservation Up," 4. See also "Indian Problems Inherited," *Lincoln Sunday Journal and Star*, December 28, 1958, 3-B.

23. Robert Agee, "Many Omahas Now Omahans," *Omaha World-Herald Magazine*, July 1, 1956, 16.

24. *1975–76 Hearings*, pt. 1, p. 49.

25. *1975–76 Hearings*, pt. 2, p. 706.

26. C. M. Dillenberg, interview with Alfred Gilpin, May 12, 1977, audiotape, American Indian Oral History Project, Department of History, University of Nebraska–Omaha.

27. Joy Miller, "Omahas Take Control of Tribe Rehabilitation," *Omaha World-Herald*, September 2, 1958, 2.

28. "Law Enforcement Conference Held Here December 3–4," *Walthill Citizen*, December 11, 1958, 1. Other news articles discussing the efforts to improve the Thurston County situation include "'Remarkable Change' in Indian Situation," *Lincoln Sunday Journal and Star*, May 18, 1958, 3-D, describing the We Shake Hands project; "Reservation Law Problems Meeting Set," *Lincoln Star*,

November 12, 1958, 21; "Indians, Officials Meet This Week to Talk Law Enforcement Problems," *Lincoln Star*, December 1, 1958, 3; "Joint Group to Study Indians' Law Problems," *Lincoln Star*, December 4, 1958, 29; and "Law Enforcement Study Unit Picked," *Lincoln Star*, December 5, 1958, 3.

29. LaVerne Madigan quoted in Earl Dyer, "Question Said 'Whether Indian Communities Can Survive,' Authority Uses Omaha Tribe as Example of Problems Here," *Lincoln Star*, September 16, 1957, 7.

30. "Bill Proposes Tribal Vote, Omaha Reservation Is Called Lawless," *Omaha World-Herald*, February 22, 1961, 3. Olsen's full statement may be found in the *Congressional Record* (February 22, 1961), 107:2576.

31. See "Seven Macy Men Charged with Rape," *Walthill Citizen*, July 31, 1969; and "Hearing Set in 'Kidnap' Case," *Omaha World-Herald*, August 1, 1969, 11. The seven Indians charged in the rape were Wayne Goham, William Cayou, Everett Bexter, Levi Levering, Thomas Davis, Victor Robinson, and Dennis Tyndall.

32. "Seek Equal Rights," *Pender Times*, July 31, 1969, 1.

33. "Hearing Set in 'Kidnap' Case," *Omaha World-Herald*, August 1, 1969, 11.

34. "Peace Pipe Board Favored for Walthill Dispute," *Omaha World-Herald*, August 7, 1969, 4.

35. "Peace Pipe Board Favored for Walthill Dispute," 4.

36. "Editor Intimidated," *Walthill Citizen*, January 15, 1970, 1.

37. "Thurston County Jail Scene of Disturbance," *Walthill Citizen*, February 12, 1970, 1.

38. "Vandals Set Fires at Macy," *Walthill Citizen*, February 12, 1970, 1.

39. See *State v Goham*, 187 Neb. 35, 187 N.W.2d. 305 (1971), *cert. denied*, 414 U.S. 834, 94 S. Ct. 174 (1971), where Wayne Goham appealed his conviction to the Nebraska Supreme Court, arguing, among other things, that the penalty imposed by the trial court had been excessive, that the state court did not have jurisdiction, and that he had received inadequate counsel. The court partly agreed, reducing Goham's penalty on the kidnapping conviction from life imprisonment to thirty-five years. The court rejected all Goham's other arguments. The court's ruling on the jurisdictional issue was particularly significant, as will be discussed below.

40. Santiago, "Indian, White Chasm Widens," 16-B.

41. Santiago, "Indian, White Chasm Widens," 16-B. Once again, the tension

on the Omaha reservation gained national notoriety. An article distributed on the *New York Times* Wire Service in July 1970 detailed the rape incident and ensuing animosity and concluded that relations between whites and Indians in the community were "still strained; very few families socialize" (Homer Bigart, "Omahas, Winnebagos Shocked at Outpouring of Prejudice," *Lincoln Star,* July 19, 1970, 4-B).

42. "Omahas Go to Powwow, Take Support of Bills to Congressmen," *Omaha World-Herald,* June 22, 1965.

43. U.S. Senate, 89th Cong., 2d sess., August 30, 1966, S. Rept. 1553, 8.

44. The circumstances leading to the passage of the Indian Bill of Rights were significantly more complex than suggested here. For additional details, see Wunder, *"Retained by the People,"* 132–40, and the sources cited therein.

45. *U.S. Statutes at Large* 82 (April 11, 1968): 77–81. Codified at 25 U.S.C. sec. 1323 (1968). The italicized language would prove to be crucial in later judicial interpretations of the statute vis-à-vis the Omaha situation.

46. Area Staff Officer's Report to Winnebago Agency Superintendent, February 7, 1969, Winnebago Agency Records, National Archives, box 103, file "Law and Order, 1961–1969."

47. Omaha Tribal Resolution 69-33, January 29, 1969.

48. Thurston County Sheriff Clyde Storie to the President, May 6, 1969; Winnebago Agency Records, National Archives, box 103, file "Law and Order, 1961–1969."

49. *1975–76 Hearings,* pt. 2, pp. 499–502. Although these hearings took place in 1976 and specifically related to the issue of retrocession for the Winnebagos, they accurately reflect the local non-Indian opposition to retrocession generally, bolstered by six years of experience with the Omahas' retrocession. Portions of this non-Indian testimony are described in Mary Kay Quinlan, "Indian Law Bills Opposed by State," *Omaha World-Herald,* March 5, 1976, 3.

50. Nebraska Legislative Council Study Committee on Indian Affairs, No. 173, Winnebago Agency Records, National Archives, box 103, file "Law and Order 1961–1969," 5.

51. Legislative Resolution 37, April 16, 1969, *Nebraska Legislative Journal,* 1969, pp. 1467–68. See also Ken Neundorf, "Indian Law Enforcement Changing," *Lincoln Star,* February 28, 1970, 14, in which Attorney General Meyer is quoted as saying, "I believe this [retrocession] is the one chance the state, the tribes, and the federal government have to resolve this situation."

131

52. Executive Order 11435, "Designating Secretary of Interior to Accept Retrocession of Jurisdiction by State," *Federal Register* 33 (November 21, 1968): 17339.

53. Memorandum of Area Special Officer William F. Walker to Area Director Re: Visit to the Omaha Reservation Regarding Nebraska's Offer of Retrocession, August 1, 1969, Winnebago Agency Records, National Archives, box 103, file "Law and Order, 1961–1969."

54. Lyndon B. Johnson, "Special Message to Congress on the Problems of the American Indian: 'The Forgotten American,'" *Congressional Record* (March 6, 1968), 114:5394–98.

55. For more on the Nixon administration's implementation of self-determination, see Wunder, *"Retained by the People,"* 159–66, and the sources cited therein.

56. Winnebago Tribal Resolution 69-19, Winnebago Agency Records, National Archives, box 103, file "Law and Order, 1961–1969." In 1865, the United States purchased the northern portion of what was then the Omaha reservation from the Omahas and ceded it to the Winnebagos, creating the Winnebago reservation. At the time the Omahas were seeking retrocession, the Winnebagos felt that, despite the problems they were incurring under PL 280, they were not yet ready to assume tribal jurisdiction. In fact, Winnebago tribal chairman Gordon Beaver indicated on one occasion that he felt that retrocession would be a "step backward" for his tribe (Neundorf, "Indian Law Enforcement Changing," 14). That attitude would change within several years, but the Winnebagos did not finally obtain retrocession until 1986 (see Statement of Louis LaRose, Winnebago Tribal Chairman, *1975–76 Hearings*, pt. 1, pp. 109–10). For detailed insight into the debate surrounding Winnebago retrocession, see Charles F. Wilkinson, "Civil Liberties Guarantees When Indian Tribes Act as Majority Societies: The Case of the Winnebago Retrocession," *Creighton Law Review* 21, no. 3 (1987–88): 773–99.

57. Walter J. Hickel, Secretary of the Interior, "Omaha Indian Reservation, Nebr.—Notice of Acceptance of Retrocession of Jurisdiction," *Federal Register* 35 (October 16, 1970): 16598.

58. "Jurisdiction Dispute Holds Up Law and Order Grant for Omaha Indians," *Omaha World-Herald*, August 26, 1970, 33.

59. Santiago, "Indian, White Chasm Widens," 16-B.

60. "Jurisdiction Dispute," 33.

61. Tom Allen, "First Indian Judge Awaits Courthouse," *Omaha World-Herald*, November 22, 1970, 1-B.

62. "Omaha Tribe Heads Believe Own Court Sign of Good Times," *Omaha World-Herald*, August 1, 1971, 18-B.

63. Legislative Resolution 16, February 1, 1971, *Nebraska Legislative Journal*, 1971, 274.

64. *State v Goham*, 187 Neb. 35, 187 N.W.2d. 305 (1971), *cert. denied*, 414 U.S. 834, 94 S. Ct. 174 (1971). As previously noted (see n. 39 above), this case involved the appeal of one of the Omaha tribal members who had been convicted and sentenced to life imprisonment in the 1969 kidnapping and rape incident. Goham argued that, because retrocession had occurred while his case was still pending in the state courts, the state had lost jurisdiction. The same argument was raised by the other Indian sentenced to life imprisonment, Dennis Tyndall, on numerous occasions. These issues bounced back and forth in the state and federal courts for over a decade. For a useful overview of what the federal district court would ultimately call a "uniquely long and complicated" series of decisions, see Judge Warren Urbom's opinion in *Tyndall v Gunter*, 681 F. Supp. 641 (D. Neb. 1987).

65. *State v Goham*, 187 N.W.2d 305, 312 (1971).

66. Commissioner of Indian Affairs Louis R. Bruce to Gordon C. Beaver, Winnebago Tribal Chairman, October 30, 1969, Winnebago Agency Records, National Archives, box 103, file "Law and Order, 1961–1969."

67. *Omaha Tribe of Nebraska v Village of Walthill*, 334 F. Supp. 823, 833 (D. Neb. 1971).

68. *Omaha Tribe of Nebraska v Village of Walthill*, 460 F.2d 1327 (8th Cir. 1972).

69. *Village of Walthill v Omaha Tribe of Nebraska*, 409 U.S. 1107, 93 S. Ct. 898 (1973).

70. The "highways exception" remains confusing and problematic on the reservation even to this day. Ed Zendejas, a tribal member and former tribal judge, reports that jurisdictional issues are "still a mess today, especially regarding the highway exception" (Ed Zendejas, interview with the author, September 14, 1995).

71. See, e.g., *Oliphant v Suquamish Indian Tribe*, 435 U.S. 191, 98 S. Ct. 655 (1978), in which the U.S. Supreme Court held that tribal courts do not possess criminal jurisdiction over non-Indians, and *Duro v Reina*, 495 U.S. 676, 110 S. Ct. 2053 (1990), holding that tribal courts do not have criminal jurisdiction

over nonmember Indians. See also, to the same effect, *Greywater v Joshua*, 846 F.2d 486 (8th Cir. 1988). Even before *Greywater* and *Duro*, however, the Omaha tribal court did not exercise authority over non-Omaha Indians, compounding the law enforcement confusion on the reservation.

72. Not surprisingly, this problem would continue to plague the reservation for many years. In 1985, a Walthill bar owner whose establishment had been burglarized complained that neither police force was investigating the crime. Sheriff Storie claimed that his hands were tied because Indians had been the culprits. The tribal police captain asserted that he had been unable to identify the suspects because Storie refused to provide any information (see Jane Juffer Sullivan, "Disagreements Loom over Jurisdiction of Crimes: Indians Want to Set Laws of the Land," *Omaha World-Herald*, July 21, 1985, 1-B).

73. Memorandum from Agency Special Officer to All Participants, April 8, 1975, Winnebago Agency Records, National Archives, box 103 (92C0007), file "Law Enforcement Meeting, 3–14–75," 2.

74. Agency Special Officer Eugene H. Trottier to Thurston County Sheriff Clyde Storie, April 1, 1975, Winnebago Agency Records, National Archives, box 103 (92C0007), file "Law Enforcement Meeting, 3–14–75."

75. Sheriff Clyde Storie to Eugene Trottier, April 6, 1975, Winnebago Agency Records, National Archives, box 103 (92C0007), file "Law Enforcement Meeting, 3–14–75."

76. Memorandum from Agency Special Officer to All Participants, April 8, 1975, Winnebago Agency Records, National Archives, box 103 (92C0007), file "Law Enforcement Meeting, 3–14–75."

77. Statement of Ralph H. Gillan, Assistant Attorney General, State of Nebraska, *1975–76 Hearings*, pt. 2, p. 471.

78. *1975–76 Hearings*, 565. Anne Flicker's status as a lightning rod for white resentment of the jurisdictional problems in Thurston County continued for years. In April 1977, another of her strident editorials angered the Omahas, bringing the threat of another Indian boycott of Walthill businesses. She wrote, "How long is the free flow of federal dollars going to last? How long is the sucker taxpayer going to believe we've mistreated and cheated the Indians at the price he is paying in taxes? We are, after all, citizens of the same United States, even though many Indians deny the fact" (see Tom Allen, "Editor to Ease Comments after Indian Boycott Threat," *Omaha World-Herald*, April 24, 1977, 22B).

79. *1975–76 Hearings*, pt. 2, pp. 499–500.

80. Sullivan, "Indians Want to Set Laws of the Land," 1-B (Storie), 6-B (Concerned Citizen's Council).

81. For an analysis of jurisdictional issues relating to retrocession in the context of a specific criminal proceeding on the Omaha reservation, see Peter T. Suzuki, "Retrocession and Jurisdictional Issues Facing the Omaha Tribe of Nebraska," *Man and Life: Journal of the Institute of Social Research and Applied Anthropology* 18 (January–June 1992): 1–10.

82. Sullivan, "Indians Want to Set Laws of the Land," 1-B.

83. *1975–76 Hearings*, pt. 1, pp. 49–50.

3. Omaha Experience with ICC Case 225

1. A complete examination of the insufficiencies of the pre-ICC Indian claims process is beyond my scope here. Generally speaking, however, the creation of the U.S. Court of Claims in 1855 initially opened the door for the prosecution of certain types of claims against the federal government that previously had been barred by the doctrine of sovereign immunity. In 1863, however, Congress closed even this limited avenue of relief to Indians by amending the Court of Claims Act to exclude from its jurisdiction claims based on violation of Indian treaties. Thereafter, Indian tribes could pursue claims against the government only by the passage of a special congressional act specifically allowing that particular litigation. For obvious reasons, such a system proved inequitable and ultimately unsatisfactory. Comprehensive analysis of these problems is available in numerous sources, including the seminal 1928 Meriam Report and several modern commentaries (see, e.g., Meriam and Roe Cloud, *The Problem of Indian Administration*, 805–11; Wunder, "Retained by the People," 89–91; and Canby, *American Indian Law*, 264–68).

2. Indian Claims Commission Act of 1946, *U.S. Statutes at Large* 60 (August 13, 1946): 1049–56 (hereafter ICC Act of 1946).

3. The commission was originally designed to remain in operation for only ten years, with all claims to be filed within the first five years (ICC Act of 1946, secs. 12, 23). In the light of the large volume of claims filed and the extraordinary demands of the commission's work, its life was repeatedly extended by Congress, which allowed it finally to expire only in 1978.

4. Despite its amply documented failings, even the most bitter of the ICC's

135

critics must concede that the commission did provide a viable, albeit imperfect, mechanism for Indians to prosecute a wide variety of claims against the government. Virtually every recognized Indian group in the country took advantage of the opportunity. By the time of its extinction in 1978, the commission had heard and decided almost five hundred separately docketed claims, with the Indian claimants winning awards in 58 percent of them (Harvey Rosenthal, "Indian Claims and the American Conscience," in *Irredeemable America: The Indians' Estate and Land Claims,* ed. Imre Sutton [Albuquerque: University of New Mexico Press, 1985], 67). The total amount awarded by the commission during its lifetime is a matter of some dispute among the ICC commentators. For example, Donald Fixico asserts that the awards totaled $669 million, Rosenthal estimates the figure to be "some $800 million," while Francis Paul Prucha sets the amount at "more than $818 million" (Fixico, *Termination and Relocation,* 186; Rosenthal, "Indian Claims and the American Conscience," 67; Francis Paul Prucha, *The Great Father: The United States Government and the American Indians,* 2 vols. [Lincoln: University of Nebraska Press, 1984], 2:1022). Whatever the precise figure, Prucha's observation that the ICC awards did at least provide "a sizable injection of money into the tribal economies, even though the lasting effects of the sum were not great," seems to be a reasonable and objective view (*The Great Father,* 2:1022).

5. Harry S. Truman, Statement upon Signing of the Indian Claims Commission Act of 1946, August 13, 1946, in *Public Papers of the Presidents of the United States: Harry S. Truman, 1946* (Washington DC: U.S. Government Printing Office, 1962), 414.

6. This conclusion is almost universal among the ICC analysts (see, e.g., Prucha, *The Great Father,* 2:1022–23; and Wunder, *"Retained by the People,"* 91–93). Whatever doubt may have existed about the shift in the ICC's philosophical underpinnings evaporated in 1960, when Arthur Watkins was appointed to the commission. Wunder accurately refers to Watkins as the "godfather of the termination policy" (*"Retained by the People,"* 112). In some instances, ICC awards were used virtually to extort tribal acceptance of termination (see Robert C. Carriker, "The Kalispel Tribe and the Indian Claims Commission Experience," *Western Historical Quarterly* 9 [January 1978]: 19–31, describing Senator Frank Church's attempts to have the ICC's award to the Kalispels withheld until the tribe agreed on a plan of termination).

7. Rosenthal's work is by far the most comprehensive examination of the legislative history and operation of the ICC (see Harvey D. Rosenthal, "Their Day in Court: A History of the Indian Claims Commission" [Ph.D. diss., Kent State

University, 1976]; an abridged and updated version of his findings may be found in his "Indian Claims and the American Conscience"). In addition to Rosenthal's work and that of Prucha (*The Great Father*), Wunder (*"Retained by the People"*), and Fixico (*Termination and Relocation*), generalized examinations of the icc may be found in many other sources, including Wilcomb Washburn, *Red Man's Land/White Man's Law: A Study of the Past and Present Status of the American Indian* (New York: Scribner's, 1971), 101–53; and Vine Deloria Jr., "'Congress in Its Wisdom': The Course of Indian Legislation," in Cadwalader and Deloria, eds., *The Aggressions of Civilization*, 105–30. Representative journal articles include Sandra Danforth, "Repaying Historical Debts: The Indian Claims Commission," *North Dakota Law Review* 49 (winter 1973): 359–403; John T. Vance, "The Congressional Mandate and the Indian Claims Commission," *North Dakota Law Review* 45 (spring 1969): 325–36; Thomas Le Duc, "The Work of the Indian Claims Commission under the Act of 1946," *Pacific Historical Review* 26 (February 1957): 1–16; and Nancy O. Lurie, "The Indian Claims Commission," *Annals of the American Academy of Political and Social Science* 436 (March 1978): 97–110.

8. Prucha is representative of the former sentiments, concluding that "the work of the Indian Claims Commission was a mixture of positive results and substantial failure" (*The Great Father*, 2:1022). Wunder is representative of the latter, calling the icc a "self-defeating" institution and "a miserable failure for Native Americans" (*"Retained by the People,"* 114).

9. Although such localized examinations are relatively rare, a few are available, including Herbert Hoover, "Yankton Sioux Tribal Claims against the United States, 1917–1975," *Western Historical Quarterly* 7 (April 1976): 125–42; Carriker, "The Kalispel Tribe and the Indian Claims Commission Experience"; and David J. Wishart, "The Pawnee Claims Case, 1947–64," in Sutton, ed., *Irredeemable America*.

10. One of the original three icc commissioners was an attorney from Nebraska, William M. Holt. Holt would serve on the commission for twenty-one years—longer than any other person. John Wunder has argued that Holt and the other two first commissioners "were chosen precisely because they lacked experience in Indian law" (*"Retained by the People,"* 111). For much more on Holt, see Francis Moul, "William McKinley Holt and the Indian Claims Commission," *Great Plains Quarterly* 16 (summer 1996): 169–81.

11. The act is silent on this point. The commission itself chose to limit its remedial powers to monetary awards. This aspect of the commission's limitations is

considered in virtually all the ICC commentaries, but see esp. Richard A. Nielsen, "American Indian Land Claims: Land versus Money as a Remedy," *University of Florida Law Review* 25 (winter 1973): 308–26.

12. The commission's determination that it could not award interest on its awards to Indians has been the subject of substantial scholarly attention. Most commentators suggest that simple political expediency was behind the decision, concluding that the ICC was "trying to avoid paying large, politically unacceptable claims" (Leonard A. Carlson, "What Was It Worth? Economic and Historical Aspects of Determining Awards in Indian Land Claims Cases," in Sutton, ed., *Irredeemable America*, 98; see also Howard M. Friedman, "Interest on Indian Claims: Judicial Protection of the Fisc," *Valparaiso University Law Review* 5 [fall 1970]: 26–47). Others have pointed to the effect of the Court of Claims decision in *Loyal Band or Group of Creek Indians v United States*, 97 F. Supp 426 (Ct. Cl. 1951), and the Supreme Court's decisions in *United States v Alcea Band of Tillamooks*, 341 U.S. 48 (1951), and *Tee-Hit-Ton Indians v United States*, 348 U.S. 273 (1955). In the latter, the Court held that, in the absence of statutory direction, the taking of Indian land was not compensable under the Fifth Amendment and that no interest was therefore due (see Le Duc, "The Work of the Indian Claims Commission," 14; and Wunder, "*Retained by the People*," 113–14).

13. For analysis of the commission's position on the question of valuation, see Carlson, "What Was It Worth?"

14. The "offset problem" is noted and discussed in virtually all the ICC treatments previously cited, including Rosenthal ("Indian Claims and the American Conscience"), Prucha (*The Great Father*), Wunder (*"Retained by the People"*), and DeLoria ("'Congress in Its Wisdom'"). For a specific examination of certain aspects of the offset issue, see John R. White, "Barmecide Revisited: The Gratuitous Offset in Indian Claims Cases," *Ethnohistory* 25 (spring 1978): 179.

15. As with other elements of the ICC story, the commission's procedural operations have been thoroughly examined in the secondary literature. A particularly concise description of the commission's processing of claims may be found in Rosenthal, "Their Day in Court," 157–58.

16. The records of the ICC have been compiled on microfiche by the Clearwater Publishing Co., New York, with the documents segmented into six "parts" and organized by docket number. Part A comprises commission decisions; pts. B and C cover transcripts of testimony; pt. D is titled *Briefs* and includes the

138

pleadings, motions, and proposed findings filed by the parties; pt. E contains General Services Administration materials relating to the claims, such as the texts of relevant treaties; and pt. F, labeled *Journal,* contains the commission's dockets and interlocutory orders entered in each claim. Subsequent citations to those records will be to ICC, with appropriate references to the "part" of the fiche collection, the title of the document, the date, the page or paragraph, and the particular microfiche card or cards on which the document may be found.

17. ICC, Docket 225, Briefs, Complaint, August 8, 1951, par. 12, card 1. Although this portion of the complaint specifies only the July 20, 1815, Portage des Sioux and October 6, 1825, Fort Atkinson treaties, those agreements did not actually result in the cession of any Omaha lands. It may be presumed therefore that these allegations were primarily directed toward the July 15, 1830, Prairie du Chien Treaty and the October 15, 1836, Platte Purchase agreement between the Omahas and the federal government. For a comprehensive examination of the execution and effect of these treaties, see Boughter, *Betraying Their Trust,* chaps. 1–2.

18. ICC, Docket 225, Briefs, Complaint, August 8, 1951, par. 14, card 1.

19. ICC, Docket 225, Briefs, Complaint, August 8, 1951, pars. 16, 15, card 1.

20. For an excellent discussion of the circumstances surrounding the 1854 treaty and its effect on the Omahas, see Boughter, *Betraying the Omaha Nation,* chap. 3.

21. ICC, Docket 225, Briefs, Complaint, August 8, 1951, pars. 22, 26, card 1.

22. ICC, Docket 225, Briefs, Complaint, August 8, 1951, par. 28, card 1. One of the tribal members killed by the Sioux in the period immediately following the 1854 treaty was the noted leader Logan Fontanelle (see Boughter, *Betraying the Omaha Nation,* chap. 3).

23. ICC, Docket 225, Briefs, Complaint, August 8, 1951, pars. 29, 36, card 1.

24. ICC, Docket 225, Journal, Commission Interlocutory Order, October 6, 1953, card 7.

25. ICC, Docket 225-B, Briefs, Amended Complaint, October 6, 1953, card 1.

26. ICC, Docket 225-C, Briefs, Amended Complaint, October 30, 1958, card 1. The allegations of Case 225-C were later amended again, becoming Docket 225-D.

27. The full text of the 1854 treaty may be found at *U.S. Statutes at Large* 10 (March 16, 1854): 1043; and in Charles J. Kappler, comp. and ed., *Indian Affairs: Laws and Treaties* (Washington DC: U.S. Government Printing Office, 1904),

2:611. Relevant portions of the treaty are quoted in the Omahas' amended complaint in docket 225-A.

28. The circumstances surrounding the Omahas' rejection of the northern lands and their choice of the territory in the Black Bird Hills is an interesting story in itself. The tribe apparently had little, if any, intention of ever accepting the land north of the Aoway line (see Boughter, *Betraying the Omaha Nation*, chap. 3).

29. *U.S. Statutes at Large* 36 (June 22, 1910): 580.

30. *Omaha Tribe of Indians v United States*, 53 Ct. Cl. 549 (1918), *rev'd in part and aff'd in part*, 253 U.S. 275 (1920).

31. *United States v Omaha Tribe of Indians*, 253 U.S. 275 (1920). The Supreme Court denied the Omahas' request for interest on this award, holding that interest could be awarded only if the special jurisdictional act allowing the lawsuit specifically provided for it. Five years later, however, Congress passed special legislation providing for the payment of interest at 5 percent on the award, totaling $374,465.02 (see *U.S. Statutes at Large* 43 [February 9, 1925]: 820; and *U.S. Statutes at Large* 44 [March 3, 1926]: 174).

32. ICC, Docket 225-A, Journal, Interlocutory Order, October 19, 1954, card 8.

33. Although he was subjected to brief cross-examination by counsel for the Omahas, Smith's testimony before the commission took the form of a written report, entered as Defendant's Exhibit 100 in Docket 225-A. The microfiche copy of his report is of very poor quality and is virtually unreadable. Perhaps for that reason, it has been separately published in hardback form as G. Hubert Smith, *Omaha Indians: Ethnohistorical Report on the Omaha People* (New York: Garland, 1974). Champe's testimony on both direct and cross-examination stretched over two days of hearings before the commission. His research and opinions are available only through examination of the official ICC transcripts (see ICC, Docket 225-A, Transcript, September 27–28, 1955, cards 1–3).

34. Smith, *Omaha Indians*, 131.

35. ICC, Transcript, Docket 225-A, card 2, pp. 139–40.

36. ICC, Transcript, Docket 225-A, card 1, p. 26.

37. ICC, Journal, Docket 225-A, Opinion, January 18, 1957, card 8. The commission's opinion may also be found in Smith, *Omaha Indians*, 280–86.

38. The Omahas had argued that their title was established, not only by their use and occupancy of the property in question, but also by the actions of the

government in acknowledging their ownership at the time the 1854 treaty was executed. Having been persuaded by Champe's testimony regarding the Omahas' use and occupancy of the territory, the commission noted that it was unnecessary to rule on that alternative basis for establishing title (Smith, *Omaha Indians*, 285).

39. The increase from 4.5 to more than 4.9 million acres reflected the commission's determination of the correct amount of land ceded by the Omahas, *including* the territory north of the Aoway line.

40. The transcript of the February 24–27, 1958, valuation hearing is found at ICC, Transcript, Docket 225-A, cards 4–8. Future researchers should note that several of the 225-A "Transcript" microfiche cards have been mistitled by the publisher. Each of the eight cards is labeled "Title" and dated "9/27/55," indicating that all eight relate to the September 1955 hearing on the issue of ownership. Actually, only cards 1–3 contain the 1955 *title* hearing. Cards 4–8 are the transcript of the 1958 *valuation* hearing.

41. Murray's oral testimony before the commission is at ICC, Transcript, Docket 225-A, cards 7–8. His written report is included in the ICC records at ICC, Testimony, Docket 225-A, W. G. Murray Appraisal, cards 1–2. It has also been separately published as William G. Murray, *Appraisal of Omaha Tract in Nebraska, 1854* (New York: Clearwater, 1957).

42. Murray, *Appraisal of Omaha Tract*, 131.

43. Davis's oral testimony before the commission is at ICC, Transcript, Docket 225-A, cards 4–6, pp. 294–494. His six-hundred-page written report, comprising thirty microfiche cards, is found at ICC, Testimony, Docket 225-A, Appraisal Associates, cards 1–30.

44. ICC, Testimony, Docket 225-A, Appraisal Associates, card 1.

45. For unknown reasons, the November 28, 1958, decision is not included in the microfiche records of Case 225. It may be found, however, in the official reports of the commission's decisions, at 6 Ind. Cl. Comm. 730 (1958).

46. ICC, Journal, Docket 225-A, "Conclusions of Law and Final Award," May 6, 1959, card 11. See also ICC, Journal, Docket 225-A, "Opinion on Orders Disallowing a Claim of Defendant as to Credit or Offset for $374,465.02," May 13, 1959, card 11. This opinion explains the commission's decision regarding the claimed offset.

47. Inexplicably, the microfiche records of the pleadings, motions, and other filings by the parties in Case 225 conclude with documents filed on October 29,

1958, more than one year before the filing of the joint "Stipulation of Settlement." Thus, the precise wording of the parties' original agreement is unavailable. The terms of the compromise may, however, be gleaned from the commission's subsequent opinion, in which it accepted the compromise and incorporated the parties' agreement into its final judgment (8 Ind. Cl. Comm. 392 [1960]).

48. 8 Ind. Cl. Comm. 392, at 414 (1960).

49. 8 Ind. Cl. Comm. 392, at 416–18 (1960).

50. ICC, Docket 225 Consolidated, Journal, Final Judgment of Final Determination, February 11, 1960, card 12.

51. ICC, Docket 225 Consolidated, Journal, Order Allowing Attorney Fees and Expenses, February 11, 1960, card 12. The attorneys' fees were based on a contract with the Omahas calling for an 8 percent fee on the commission's final award.

52. Rosenthal, "Their Day in Court," 297.

53. For discussion of this larger issue, see Rosenthal, "Their Day in Court," 297–99.

54. Resolution of Omaha Tribal Council, March 8, 1961 (full text contained in U.S. Senate, *Providing for the Disposition of Judgment Funds of the Omaha Tribe of Indians*, 87th Cong., 1st sess., 1961, S. Rept. 598 [ser. set 12324]).

55. Public Law 87-235, *U.S. Statutes at Large* 75 (September 14, 1961): 508.

56. "3,000 Share Tribe Award," *Omaha World-Herald*, January 14, 1962, 6-B.

57. Ed Zendejas, interview with the author, September 14, 1995.

58. "Omaha Indians Receive Tribal Claims Money," *Walthill Citizen*, June 14, 1962, 1.

59. Harold Cowan, "Omahas Use $750 Shares to Pay Off Debts, Buy Bikes," *Omaha World-Herald*, June 17, 1962, 1-B.

60. Tom Allan, "Indians at Macy Build and Plan," *Omaha World-Herald*, September 29, 1962, 4. See also Tom Allan, "Indians' Progress Pleases 'Big White Father,'" *Omaha World-Herald*, June 26, 1964, 6-B.

61. The Omahas' use of their ICC judgment fund is described and favorably evaluated in U.S. Senate, *Providing for the Disposition of Funds Appropriated to Pay a Judgment in Favor of the Omaha Tribe of Nebraska, and for Other Purposes*, 89th Cong., 2d sess., 1966, S. Rept. 1683 (ser. set 12710-5) (hereafter cited as S. Rept. 1683). See also "Reservation Gets Factory; Indians at Walthill Use Federal Money," *Omaha World-Herald*, October 15, 1967, 12-A.

62. S. Rept. 1683, 3.

63. "Omaha Tribe Given Praise, Nash Lauds Efforts to Boost Economy," *Omaha World-Herald*, August 20, 1962, 2.

64. "Indians Plan a Delegation, Want to Give View of Off-Reservation," *Omaha World-Herald*, October 21, 1961, 2.

65. See Tom Allan, "Omaha Tribe's Crucial Day Nov. 5," *Omaha World-Herald*, October 4, 1962, 6, describing the results of the primary election as "a tough blow to the incumbent council," and assessing the import of the November 5 general election; and Tom Allan, "Old Council Is Voted Out," *Omaha World-Herald*, November 6, 1962, 6, discussing the results of the general election.

66. James Ivey, "Indians Declare Macy Council Discriminates," *Omaha World-Herald*, September 21, 1963, 2.

67. At the time of the ICC distribution, Article II of the Omaha constitution merely provided that all persons "of Indian blood" whose names appeared on tribal rolls were entitled to membership (see "Constitution and By-Laws of the Omaha Tribe of Nebraska," March 30, 1936, Art. II, sec. 1, reprinted in George E. Fay, comp., *Charters, Constitutions and By-Laws of the Indian Tribes of North America*, pt. 13, *Midwestern Tribes*, Occasional Publications in Anthropology, Ethnology Series, no. 14 (Greeley: Museum of Anthropology, University of Northern Colorado, 1972), 49–58.

68. See "Indians Schedule Walthill Meeting," *Omaha World-Herald*, August 9, 1962, 19; and "Indians Not on Rolls Seek Fund Injunction," *Omaha World-Herald*, August 20, 1962, 2.

69. Such fragmentation was not uncommon among tribes receiving ICC awards (see Carriker, "The Kalispel Tribe and the Indian Claims Commission Experience," describing the Kalispels' similar problems).

4. Round Two before the ICC

1. Statement of Attorney Lawrence C. Mills in Closing Arguments, ICC, Docket 138, Transcript, card 13, p. 1154.

2. For discussion of the modern criticism heaped on the ICC, see nn. 4, 6–8, in chap. 3 above.

3. The treaties discussed herein can be found in numerous sources, including *Statutes at Large* for the year in which each treaty was ratified. Francis Paul Prucha's *American Indian Treaties: The History of a Political Anomaly* (Berkeley:

University of California Press, 1994) covers the negotiation and execution of the long series of treaties with the tribes of the Upper Midwest in the early decades of the nineteenth century (see pp. 135–43, 198–201). Probably the most accessible source for the treaties is Kappler, comp. and ed., *Indian Affairs*, vol. 2, which I in fact use in this chapter.

4. Kappler, comp. and ed., *Indian Laws and Treaties*, 2:250–55.

5. There is some confusion in the records regarding references to the August 1825 agreement. While the treaty itself indicates that it was executed at "Prairie des Chiens," some modern commentaries refer to the site as "Prairie du Chien." References to the 1825 treaty in icc pleadings add to the confusion by varying between the two spellings. The issue is further clouded by the subsequent execution of the seminal 1830 treaty, wherein the site is explicitly acknowledged as "Prairie du Chien" in both the treaty itself and all commentaries. I will refer to the 1825 agreement as the "Prairie des Chiens" Treaty to distinguish it from the 1830 agreement, the "Prairie du Chien" Treaty.

6. The Omahas did enter into a separate agreement with the United States several months later at Fort Atkinson (see Kappler, comp. and ed., *Indian Laws and Treaties*, 2:260–62). In that treaty, the tribe "acknowledged the supremacy and claimed the protection" of the United States. For its part, the federal government agreed to extend to the Omahas "such benefits and acts of kindness as may be convenient." That treaty of comity did not address any of the land issues involved in the Prairie des Chiens agreement.

7. icc, Docket 138, "Brief of Omaha Petitioners in Support of Proposed Findings of Fact," Briefs, card 4, p. 25 (hereafter cited as "Brief of Omahas," giving only page number). The Omahas' argument that the Sac and Fox had no recognizable interest in the land in question would be a source of ongoing cross-attacks throughout the icc litigation.

8. Kappler, comp. and ed., *Indian Laws and Treaties*, 2:253–54.

9. "Brief of Omahas," 25. In the modern era, the Mesquakie (Fox) tribe has continued to bump heads with the Omahas on the issue of gaming in the Council Bluffs, Iowa, area. For more on the Sac and Fox in Iowa, see Michael D. Green, "We Dance in Different Directions: Mesquakie (Fox) Separatism from the Sac and Fox Tribe," *Ethnohistory* 30, no. 3 (1983): 129–40.

10. Kappler, comp. and ed., *Indian Laws and Treaties*, 2:305.

11. "Indian Removal Act of 1830," *U.S. Statutes at Large* 4 (May 28, 1830): 411–12.

12. ICC, Docket 138, "Petition Relating to Lands in Western Iowa and Northwestern Missouri," Briefs, card 1 (of seven), pars. 28, 32, 29 (later allegation) (hereafter cited as "Petition").

13. "Petition," par. 31.

14. Kappler, comp. and ed., *Indian Laws and Treaties*, 2:306.

15. "Petition," par. 32.

16. For additional discussion of the negotiation and execution of the 1830 Prairie du Chien Treaty in terms of the effect on the Omahas, see Boughter, *Betraying Their Trust*, chap. 2.

17. Kappler, comp. and ed., *Indian Laws and Treaties*, 2:402–14.

18. For discussion of the political and other considerations leading to the Platte Purchase, see Boughter, *Betraying the Omaha Nation*, chap. 2; and Howard I. McKee, "The Platte Purchase," *Missouri Historical Review* 32 (January 1938): 129–47.

19. Kappler, comp. and ed., *Indian Laws and Treaties*, 2:479–80.

20. "Brief of Omahas," 25. These treaties are in Kappler, comp. and ed., *Indian Laws and Treaties*, 2:495–96, 497–98, 500–501.

21. "Brief of Omahas," 30.

22. Kappler, comp. and ed., *Indian Laws and Treaties*, 2:611. Article 3 of the 1854 treaty contains the cession of the Omahas' lands east of the Missouri River.

23. "Brief of Omahas," 31.

24. For details regarding the theories of recovery available under the ICC Act of 1946, see chap. 3 above.

25. "Petition," par. 39.

26. "Petition," par. 40.

27. ICC, Docket 138, "Answer of Defendant United States of America," Briefs, card 1, pars. 43, 45, 44.

28. ICC, Docket 138, "Answer of Defendant United States of America," Briefs, card 1, par. 44.

29. For discussion of the procedural operations of the ICC, see chap. 3 above.

30. Wallace's testimony began on the afternoon of December 7, 1954, and continued through December 8 and the morning of December 9 (see ICC, Docket 138, Transcripts, cards 1–4, pp. 75–368).

31. Wedel's testimony is at ICC, Docket 138, Transcripts, cards 4–8, pp. 376–689.

32. ICC, Docket 138, Briefs, "Objections to Other Petitioners' and Defendant's Proposed Findings of Fact and Reply to Defendant's Objections to Sac and Fox Petitioners' Proposed Findings of Fact," card 5, pp. 23–24.

33. The ICC's findings of fact and decision rendered July 31, 1957, were entered in *both* Docket 138 and Docket 11-A, the latter being the claim of the affiliated Otoe and Missouri tribes involving the same area. The two cases were thereafter consolidated for further handling.

34. ICC, Dockets 11-A and 138, Decisions, card 36, Commission Opinion, pp. 365–66.

35. ICC, Dockets 11-A and 138, Decisions, card 36, Commission Finding of Fact 50, pp. 349–50.

36. Testifying on behalf of the claimants were Dr. Thomas H. Le Duc, a historian from Oberlin College, Dr. Henry L. Krusekopf, professor emeritus of soils at the University of Missouri, and Dr. Frank F. Reicken, professor of soils at Iowa State University. With the consolidation of Dockets 138 and 11-A, the microfiche ICC transcripts relating to the valuation hearing are indexed under and located within the 11-A records. This testimony may thus be found at ICC, Docket 11-A, Transcripts, cards 1–4.

37. Murray's oral testimony is at ICC, Docket 11-A, Transcripts, cards 4–7. His written report is reproduced separately within the microfiche records at ICC, Docket 11-A, "Appraisal, W. G. Murray," cards 1–4.

38. See chap. 3 above.

39. Just as was the case with Docket 225, the actual stipulated agreement does not appear in the ICC microfiche records. The terms and conditions set out therein may be determined, however, by the transcripts of the commission's evidentiary hearing regarding the settlement and the final judgment subsequently entered by the commission.

40. For a full description of the Omaha Rule established in Docket 225, see chap. 3 above.

41. Because Dockets 138 and 11-A remained consolidated, the transcript of the March 1964 settlement hearing is indexed and located within the 11-A materials (see ICC, Docket 11-A, Transcripts, card 1, "Settlement").

42. ICC, Docket 11-A, Transcripts, card 1, "Settlement," pp. 48–50, 62–63. See

also "Omahas Accept Settlement Plan," *Omaha World-Herald*, February 15, 1964, 7; and "Tribe Accepts Claims Settlement," *Walthill Citizen*, February 20, 1964, 1.

43. For discussion of this issue, see chap. 3 above and the works cited therein.

44. icc, Docket 11-a, Transcripts, card 1, "Settlement," pp. 55–56, 64–65.

45. icc, Docket 11-a, Transcripts, card 1, "Settlement," pp. 72–73.

46. icc, Docket 138, Journal, Final Judgment, April 14, 1964, card 15.

47. See Tom Allan, "Omahas Offered $1,750,000 for Hunting Lands," *Omaha World-Herald*, January 9, 1964, 26, in which it was reported that the tribe was "rejoicing" at the news of the proposed settlement but that the joy was tempered by warnings that "it will be many a moon before the money is in the wampum bag." That same article foreshadowed the potential problems related to the distribution of the funds, noting that "controversy had raged" several years earlier over that issue.

48. Public Law 88-317, *U.S. Statutes at Large* 78 (June 9, 1964): 204–13.

49. Omaha Tribal Resolution 33-65, April 19, 1965, cited in S. Rept. 1683.

50. S. Rept. 1683, 6–7. (Anderson's full report can be found at pp. 4–15.)

51. Additional insight into Congress's review of the Omaha distribution plan may be found in U.S. House, *Providing for the Disposition of Funds Appropriated to Pay a Judgment in Favor of the Omaha Tribe*, 89th Cong., 1st sess., 1965, H. Rept. 891 (ser. set 12665-5).

52. S. Rept. 1683, 14–15.

53. *U.S. Statutes at Large* 80 (November 2, 1966): 1114–15.

54. Tom Allan, "Santa Early for Indians; But Federal Money is 112 Years Late," *Omaha World-Herald*, December 23, 1966 (evening ed.), 1. An article in the *World-Herald*'s morning edition that same day had reported the tribe's great disappointment that the checks had not been received on the previous day as had been expected (Tom Allan, "'Santa Claus' 112 Years, 1 Day Late; Tribe Still Awaiting Checks," *Omaha World-Herald*, December 23, 1966 [morning ed.], 11).

55. Fred Thomas, "Indians Plan Fall Parley; Omaha Tribe Rivals Agree to Confer," *Omaha World-Herald*, October 13, 1966, 1.

56. Fred Thomas, "Tribe Claims 'Hands Tied,'" *Omaha World-Herald*, October 15, 1966, 13.

57. See, e.g., "Indian Asking Fund Report," *Omaha World-Herald*, February 22, 1968 (evening ed.), 24, describing the filing of a lawsuit by an off-reservation member charging mismanagement of the judgment fund. The case was dismissed by the court two years later, after the plaintiff failed to appear at several scheduled hearings (see "Judge Dismisses Suit against Omaha Tribe," *Omaha World-Herald*, April 22, 1970).

58. Ed Zendejas, interview with the author, September 14, 1995.

59. See "Constitution and By-Laws of the Omaha Tribe of Nebraska," Art. V, section 1, reprinted in Fay, comp., *Charters, Constitutions and By-Laws*, 53.

60. Ed Zendejas, interview with the author, September 14, 1995.

61. See Tom Allan, "'Santa Claus' 112 Years, 1 Day Late," 11, in which Chairman Gilpin hinted that the tribe might soon initiate litigation seeking the return of land that had originally been part of the reservation but that was now on the Iowa side of the Missouri River owing to a shift in the river's channel.

5. Legal Struggle for Blackbird Bend

1. The literature on the Red Power movement is abundant. For brief overviews, see Prucha, *The Great Father*, 2:1116–21; and Wunder, *"Retained by the People,"* 156–59. Among the more detailed examinations of these events (generally told from the Indian point of view) are Paul Chaat Smith and Robert Allen Warrior, *Like a Hurricane* (New York: New Press, 1996); Peter Blue Cloud, ed., *Alcatraz Is Not an Island* (Berkeley CA: Wingbow, 1972); Robert Burnette and John Koster, *The Road to Wounded Knee* (New York: Bantam, 1974); Vine Deloria Jr., *Behind the Trail of Broken Treaties: An Indian Declaration of Independence* (New York: Delacorte, 1974); and Peter Matthiessen, *In the Spirit of Crazy Horse* (New York: Viking, 1983; reprint, Harmondsworth: Penguin, 1991).

2. Fred Thomas, "Claims Threaten Recreation Tract," *Omaha World-Herald*, February 22, 1980, 8, quoting Sheriff Albert Wood.

3. Wunder, *"Retained by the People,"* 213.

4. The *Omaha World-Herald*, the *Sioux City Journal*, the *Lincoln Star*, and the *Des Moines Register* all provided extensive coverage of the litigation. The first two in particular are frequently cited herein. In addition, Theodore Steinberg's essay "Blackbird's Ghost" (in *Slide Mountain; or, The Folly of Owning Nature* [Berkeley: University of California Press, 1995], 21–51) takes as its subject the early stages of the Blackbird Bend litigation. See also Ros Jensen, "Blackbird

Bend: Landmark Victory in Land Dispute," *Christian Century* 95, no. 21 (June 7–14, 1978): 606–8.

5. For academic analysis of this aspect of the Blackbird Bend story, see Laurie Smith Camp, "Land Accretion and Avulsion: The Battle of Blackbird Bend," *Nebraska Law Review* 56 (1977): 814–35; and Daniel Henry Ehrlich, "Problems Arising from Shifts of the Missouri River on the Eastern Border of Nebraska," *Nebraska History* 54 (fall 1973): 341–63.

6. 25 U.S.C. sec. 194 (1834).

7. See Margaret Hotopp, "Preferential Burden of Proof Allocation in Indian Land Claims Cases," *Iowa Law Review* 64 (January 1979): 386–407. See also Mark W. Thomas, "Constitutional Law—Equal Protection—Supreme Court Upholds Validity of Preferential Treatment of Indians in Land Disputes—*Wilson v Omaha Indian Tribe*," *Creighton Law Review* 13 (winter 1979): 619–32, wherein the author suggests that the statute's effect is "academically suspect but morally persuasive" (p. 632). See also Rjean K. Formanek, "Blackbird Hills Indian Land Dispute Settled by Placing the Burden of Proving Title on the Non-Indian Party and Incorporating Nebraska Water Law into the Federal Standard," *Creighton Law Review* 13 (summer 1980): 1098–1102.

8. Scholarly discussion of the recurring problems inherent in the government's ambiguous role as trustee of Indian lands is abundant and provides a useful secondary context for my discussion here (see, e.g., Robert T. Coulter and Steven M. Tullberg, "Indian Land Rights," in Cadwalader and Deloria, eds., *The Aggressions of Civilization,* 185–213, describing the trust relationship as "racial discrimination and boundless United States power disguised as moral and legal duty" [p. 198]). In his seminal work *The Great Father* (2:1202–6), Prucha laments the "murkiness" that pervades the trust relationship, clouding the already ambiguous line between Indian self-determination and federal paternalism. For a cogent synthesis of the legal bases for the trust relationship, see Canby, *American Indian Law,* 37–52.

9. The government's duty to represent the Omahas at Blackbird Bend emanates from the murky trust relationship referred to previously. Where, as here, the trustee takes an entirely different view of the issue at hand than does the beneficiary, the potential for bitter conflict is apparent.

10. "Omaha Indians Fight for Land," *Omaha World-Herald,* February 11, 1966, 7.

11. The full text of the 1854 treaty may be found in *U.S. Statutes at Large* 10 (March 16, 1854):1043; and in Kappler, comp. and ed., *Indian Affairs,* 2:611.

12. *United States v Wilson*, 433 F. Supp. 67 (N.D. Iowa 1977), Finding of Fact 4, p. 68.

13. The precise manner in which the Iowa farmers gained possession of the land is itself an elusive story. It appears that, by the early 1920s, a man named Joe Kirk had taken control of most of the property, building a log cabin and cultivating clover and alfalfa on various portions. Kirk sold off the land in 1948, and it changed hands several times thereafter until 1959, when Charles Lakin and Raymond G. Peterson took title to separate portions of the tract. In 1972, Lakin gave about a thousand acres to the state of Iowa for a recreational development and sold twenty-one hundred acres to Roy Tibbals Wilson, who was renting the land to tenant farmers at the time the litigation commenced. Further complicating the question of title was the fact that the land was not taxed in Iowa until 1969, after Lakin had commenced several "quiet title" actions against adjoining white landowners (see *Charles E. Lakin v State of Iowa, et al.*, Equity No. 17400, Monona County District Court, decree filed Nov. 15, 1963). The Omahas were not named as parties in those lawsuits and would later argue, with justification, that those judgments were not controlling on the question of the tribe's original title (see Bob Gunsolley, "Indians Occupy Land Near Onawa," *Sioux City Journal*, April 6, 1973, 1; "Nebraska Indians Claim Iowa Land; AIM Group in Onawa," *Omaha World-Herald*, April 6, 1973, 2; and Fred Thomas, "Indians, Attorneys Meet; Indians Stay," *Omaha World-Herald*, April 7, 1973, 1; see also Steinberg, *Slide Mountain*, 29–31; and *United States v Wilson*, 433 F. Supp. 67 [N.D. Iowa 1977], at 83–84).

14. The sequence of events in the federal courts will be discussed more fully in the remainder of this chapter. By way of preview, the chronology of the reported decisions is as follows: *United States v Wilson*, 433 F. Supp. 57 (N.D. Iowa 1977); *United States v Wilson*, 433 F. Supp. 67 (N.D. Iowa 1977); *Omaha Indian Tribe v Wilson*, 575 F.2d 620 (8th Cir. 1978); *Wilson v Omaha Tribe*, 442 U.S. 653 (1979); *Omaha Indian Tribe v Wilson*, 614 F.2d 1153 (8th Cir. 1980), *cert. denied* 449 U.S. 825 (1980); *United States v Wilson*, 523 F. Supp. 874 (N.D. Iowa 1981); *United States v Wilson*, 707 F.2d 304 (8th Cir. 1982), *cert. denied* 465 U.S. 1025 (1984); *United States v Wilson*, 578 F. Supp. 1191 (N.D. Iowa 1984); *Omaha Indian Tribe v Jackson*, 854 F.2d 1089 (8th Cir. 1988), *cert. denied* 490 U.S. 1090; *United States v Wilson*, 926 F.2d 725 (8th Cir. 1991); *Omaha Indian Tribe v Tract 1—Blackbird Bend Area*, 933 F.2d 1462 (8th Cir.) (per curiam), *cert. denied sub nom. Omaha Indian Tribe v Agricultural & Indus. Inv. Co.*, 502 U.S. 942 (1991); *Rupp v Omaha Tribe*, 45 F.3d 1241 (8th Cir. 1995).

15. Allan, "'Santa Claus' 112 Years, 1 Day Late," 11.

16. During the period from 1966 to 1972, tribal attention was also diverted by several other lawsuits relating to the ownership of riparian land on the reservation. In one of those cases, Victor Fontanelle, grand-nephew of famed Omaha chief Logan Fontanelle, sought title to some three hundred acres of land along the river that he claimed had accreted to his family's allotment on the reservation. Following a trial of the matter in April 1967, the federal district court for Nebraska ruled in Fontanelle's favor in 1969 (see *Fontanelle v Omaha Tribe of Nebraska*, 298 F. Supp. 855 [D. Neb. 1969]). The decision was affirmed on appeal to the Eighth Circuit Court of Appeals (*Omaha Tribe of Indians v Fontanelle*, 430 F.2d 143 [8th Cir. 1970]; see also Bill Billotte, "Land of Indians Causes Dispute," *Omaha World-Herald*, April 12, 1967 [evening ed.], 1, 6; "Ex-Councilmen Say Land Really Tribe's," *Omaha World-Herald*, April 13, 1967, 8; and "Omaha Chief's Nephew Wins River Land Case," *Omaha World-Herald*, April 13, 1969, 26-B).

In a separate matter occurring at about the same time, several Iowa farmers asserted title to land on the western side of the river within the reservation, which they claimed had shifted to the Nebraska side by the river's movement. The Omahas did not contest the Iowans' title to the land. The dispute centered on the farmers' attempts to bulldoze a road through the reservation to gain access to the site (see Fred Thomas, "Indians, Farmers Make No Peace in Land Dispute," *Omaha World-Herald*, March 23, 1968, 4).

17. Randall Moody, "Funds Asked to Study Indian Land Fuss," *Omaha World-Herald*, August 31, 1972.

18. See Gunsolley, "Indians Occupy Land Near Onawa," 1; and "Nebraska Indians Claim Iowa Land," 2.

19. The juxtaposition of the Omahas' occupation of Blackbird Bend and the resolution of the AIM occupation of Wounded Knee is starkly reflected on the front page of the April 6, 1973, *Sioux City Journal*. The lead story at the top of the page provides the paper's first report of the Omahas' action at Blackbird Bend, while an Associated Press story at the bottom of the same page is headlined "Peace Comes to Wounded Knee." For more on AIM and Wounded Knee, see Burnette and Koster, *The Road to Wounded Knee*; Deloria, *Behind the Trail of Broken Treaties*; and Matthiessen, *In the Spirit of Crazy Horse*.

20. "Nebraska Indians Claim Iowa Land," 2.

21. A quiet title action is one in which a court is asked to resolve competing claims to disputed real property. Theoretically, all parties who claim an interest

in the disputed property are notified of the action and given the opportunity to assert and prove their claims.

22. Thomas, "Indians, Attorneys Meet," 1, 6. See also Fred Thomas, "Indians Stay in Onawa, Next Move Will Be Up to Attorneys," *Omaha World-Herald*, April 10, 1973, 7.

23. "Corn Picking Brings Arrest," *Omaha World-Herald*, April 22, 1973, 1-B; "Three Indians Are Charged," *Omaha World-Herald*, April 23, 1973, 28. The latter headline is incorrect inasmuch as the two other men arrested along with Cline were white farmers Harold Swanson Jr. and Kenneth Davis, who had been hired to assist the Omahas with their farming operation on the land.

24. "3 Go to Grand Jury in Picking Incident," *Omaha World-Herald*, April 26, 1973, 14.

25. See "Court Gets Land Claim," *Omaha World-Herald*, May 7, 1973, 4; and "Judge Studying Onawa Case," *Omaha World-Herald*, May 9, 1973, 32.

26. "Court Order in Iowa Not Served to Indians," *Omaha World-Herald*, May 19, 1973, 18.

27. "Occupants Seek Funds," *Omaha World-Herald*, May 1, 1973, 30.

28. "BIA Seeks Land Opinion," *Omaha World-Herald*, May 9, 1973, 32.

29. See Omaha Tribal Resolutions 75-28 and 75-31 and "Affidavit of the Omaha Indian Tribal Council," announcing the council's unanimous endorsement of the occupation and further indicating that the action had been taken "with the full approval, knowledge, and direction of the Acting Commissioner of the Bureau of Indian Affairs, Jose A. Zuni." All three of these documents are attached as exhibits to the Omahas' "Complaint for Injunction," filed May 20, 1975, Case c75-4026, Federal District Court for Northern District of Iowa, Western Division.

30. Al Frisbie, "Omaha Indians Plan Long Stay on Disputed Farmland," *Omaha World-Herald*, April 8, 1975, 1, 4.

31. Memorandum from Solicitor Kent Frizzell to Commissioner of Indian Affairs, February 3, 1975. Although the memo is not published in the reported opinions of the Interior Department, it is attached in its entirety to the Omahas' "Complaint for Injunction," filed May 20, 1975, Case c75-4026, Federal District Court for Northern District of Iowa, Western Division (hereafter cited as "Frizzell Opinion"). See also Mary Kay Quinlan, "Interior Department Says U.S. Owns Disputed Land," *Omaha World-Herald*, April 8, 1975, 4.

32. Frizzell Opinion, 1.

33. Quinlan, "Interior Department Says," 4.

34. See "Constitution and By-Laws of the Omaha Tribe of Nebraska," Art. VIII, sec. 5, reprinted in Fay, comp. *Charters, Constitutions and By-Laws,* 54.

35. The Iowans' perspective on this and other issues in the early stages of the Blackbird Bend litigation is reflected in an untranscribed interview with an attorney representing one of the Iowa claimants (see Richard W. Peterson, interview with Peter J. Peters, January 26, 1976, audiotape, American Indian Oral History Project, Department of History, University of Nebraska–Omaha).

36. Mary Kay Quinlan, "Indians Criticize Handling of Land Dispute," *Omaha World-Herald,* May 28, 1975, 2.

37. Mary Kay Quinlan, "BIA Urges Indians to File Suit," *Omaha World-Herald,* April 9, 1975, 47.

38. "Complaint to Quiet Title and for Injunctive Relief," May 19, 1975, Case c75-4024, Federal District Court for Northern District of Iowa, Western Division.

39. Over the ensuing twenty years of court action, the tribe persistently argued that the Department of Justice had fraudulently failed to meet its trust obligations to the tribe. The Omahas repeated those allegations in countless resolutions, pleadings, motions, and briefs filed with the courts during the long history of the case. One of the earliest formal assertions of those feelings is found in Omaha Tribal Resolution 75-40, dated May 28, 1975, in which the tribal council accused the government attorneys of "gross double dealings, manipulation and abuse."

40. See "U.S. Official Defends Suit for Indians," *Omaha World-Herald,* June 3, 1975, 3.

41. Kent Frizzell to Eddie Cline, quoted in "U.S. Official Defends Suit for Indians," 3.

42. "Complaint for Injunction, for a Stay of State Court Proceedings and Other Relief," May 20, 1975, Case c75-4026, Federal District Court for Northern District of Iowa, Western Division.

43. In their complaint, the Omahas asserted that the government suit initiated on the day before had been "filed over the protests of the Omaha Tribe of Nebraska" and was "in effect a conduit to permit and allow [the Iowans] to retake possession of the lands involved" ("Complaint for Injunction, for a Stay of State Court Proceedings and Other Relief," May 20, 1975, Case c75-4026, Federal District Court for Northern District of Iowa, Western Division, par. 7).

44. "Application to Dismiss or Hold in Abeyance," June 3, 1975, Case c75-

4024, Federal District Court for Northern District of Iowa, Western Division.

45. Omaha Tribal Resolution 75-40, May 28, 1975, attached to "Application to Dismiss or Hold in Abeyance," June 3, 1975, Case c75-4024, Federal District Court for Northern District of Iowa, Western Division.

46. One of the most comprehensive summaries of the tribe's arguments on the fraud issue may be found in "Motion of Omaha Indian Tribe to Have Disqualified and to Enjoin Evan L. Hultman, United States Attorney, James J. Clear, and Successors from Further Participation in These Cases, and Memorandum in Support," November 7, 1975, Cases c75-4024, c75-4026, and c75-4067 consolidated, Federal District Court for Northern District of Iowa, Western Division.

47. Wynema Morris, interview with the author, February 5, 1997. Morris was a member of the tribal council during much of the Blackbird Bend litigation.

48. Memorandum from Martin E. Seneca Jr., director of the BIA's Office of Trust Responsibility, to Reed Chambers, associate solicitor for Indian Affairs in the Interior Department, August 9, 1976, appended to "Motion of the Omaha Indian Tribe to . . . Have the Justice Department Aligned as an Adversary in These Consolidated Cases," filed September 23, 1976, Cases c75-4024, c75-4026, and c75-4067 consolidated, Federal District Court for Northern District of Iowa, Western Division.

49. U.S. District Judge Edward McManus, "Order," June 5, 1975, Cases c75-4024 and c75-4026 consolidated, Federal District Court for Northern District of Iowa, Western Division.

50. U.S. District Judge Edward McManus, "Order," July 1, 1975, Cases c75-4024 and c75-4026 consolidated, Federal District Court for Northern District of Iowa, Western Division.

51. Notwithstanding the courts' repeated rejection of the Omahas' arguments regarding Hultman's apparent conflict of interest, it should be noted that there does indeed seem to be a prima facie appearance of such a conflict. At least one ostensibly disinterested outside party offered support for the tribe on that issue. In 1987, the National Council of Churches filed an amicus curiae (friend of the court) brief in which it argued that the Omahas' claims regarding Hultman's conflict of interest were "neither frivolous nor without merit" and that the Department of Justice had "stymied and stultified the efforts of the Tribe to act in its own behalf" (see "Motion for Leave to File, Statement of Interest and Brief Amicus Curiae of the National Council of Churches in Support of the Omaha Indian Tribe's Rule 59 Motion," June 8, 1987, Cases c75-

4024, c75-4026, and c75-4067 consolidated, Federal District Court for Northern District of Iowa, Western Division).

52. "Complaint," Case c75-4067, October 6, 1975, Federal District Court for Northern District of Iowa, Western Division.

53. Vincent Willey, interview with the author, February 21, 1997. Willey was the first president of the association.

54. Quoted in "Indians Seek 3-Generation Land," *Omaha World-Herald*, October 21, 1975, 4.

55. "River Land Feud May Go to Trial," *Omaha World-Herald*, October 24, 1975, 14.

56. "River Land Feud May Go to Trial," 14.

57. Jeff Withrow, "Indians Need Tug, Barge to Haul Harvest," *Omaha World-Herald*, October 26, 1975, 24-B.

58. District Judge Edward McManus, "Order," January 26, 1976, Case c75-4067, Federal District Court for Northern District of Iowa, Western Division.

59. District Judge Edward McManus, "Order," April 5, 1976, Cases c75-4024, c75-4026, and c75-4067 consolidated, Federal District Court for Northern District of Iowa, Western Division. The Omahas thereafter consistently referred to this important severance ruling as a *sua sponte* order, which is one issued by a court on its own volition, without a formal request from any party in the suit. Technically, the April 5 order probably should not be considered *sua sponte* since the court also ruled on several pending motions within its decree. It is true, however, that there was no pending motion for severance from any party before the court at the time.

60. The tribe's claims in Case 4067 were formally stayed by the district court in 1979, pending the outcome of the other cases. Those claims were not reactivated until June 15, 1987 (see *Omaha Indian Tribe v Tract I—Blackbird Bend Area*, 933 F.2d 1462, 1464 [8th Cir. 1991]).

61. In response to later tribal arguments regarding the propriety of Judge McManus's severance order, the Eighth Circuit Court of Appeals observed that the tribe "did not object to the district court's severance order either by motion for reconsideration, request for interlocutory relief, or in any of the subsequent appeals" (see 854 F.2d. 1094, n.5).

62. Bogue, a federal district judge in South Dakota at the time, presided at the Blackbird Bend trial by special appointment. He had been scheduled to hear

the reservation murders case in Cedar Rapids that summer but was switched off that case by the Eighth Circuit. He and McManus effectively traded duties, as McManus took over the murder trial (see Jensen, "Blackbird Bend," 607).

63. There are 3,216 pages of trial transcript and more than 150 exhibits in the trial record.

64. The doctrines of avulsion and accretion are discussed in all the reported court decisions in the Blackbird Bend cases. In addition, see Camp, "Land Accretion and Avulsion," and the numerous other sources cited therein.

65. The issue was not always as simple as this summary implies. As to the lands claimed by the tribe *outside* the Barrett survey line, the Omahas sought to show that the additional land had *accreted* to the reservation as the river moved eastward after the survey. Thus, the reservation had, at first, been *increased* in size by accretion. They then argued that the newly created land had later been left on the Iowa side by a sudden *avulsion* of the river back to the west.

66. The district court actually rendered two separate opinions. The first, *United States v Wilson*, 433 F. Supp. 57 (N.D. Iowa 1977), was a memorandum opinion in which the court resolved choice of law problems, analyzed the concepts of avulsion and accretion, and discussed the allocation of the burden of proof in the case. The second opinion, *United States v Wilson*, 433 F. Supp. 67 (N.D. Iowa 1977), contained the court's specific findings of fact and conclusions of law on the merits of the dispute.

67. *United States v Wilson*, 433 F. Supp. 67, at 89.

68. *United States v Wilson*, 433 F. Supp. 67, at 92.

69. Judge Bogue's letter to the parties, dated May 2, 1977, has been incorporated as part of the official record in Cases c75-4024 and c75-4026 consolidated, Federal District Court for Northern District of Iowa, Western Division. It is quoted and discussed in Camp, "Accretion and Avulsion," 828–29. The letter was also mentioned in the regional press accounts of the decision (see R. G. Dunlop, "Indians Lose Court Battle for Iowa Farmland," *Omaha World-Herald*, May 5, 1977, 1; "Court Rules against Indians," *Des Moines Register*, May 5, 1977, 1; and "Onawa Land Decision Goes against Indians," *Sioux City Journal*, May 5, 1977, 1).

70. "Indians Defy Court Order to Vacate," *Omaha World-Herald*, May 13, 1977, 1.

71. "Temporary Order of Stay," May 14, 1977, Eighth Circuit Court of Appeals, Cases 77-1384 and 77-1387 consolidated. See also Fred Thomas, "Indians Whoop It Up; Vacate Order Halted," *Omaha World-Herald*, May 14, 1977, 15.

72. "Order of Stay," May 24, 1977, Eighth Circuit Court of Appeals, Cases 77-1384 and 77-1387 consolidated.

73. *Omaha Indian Tribe v Wilson*, 575 F.2d 620 (8th Cir. 1978).

74. 25 U.S.C. sec. 194 (1834).

75. The Omahas had argued the controlling effect of this statute in the district court, but Judge Bogue rejected its applicability. He held that invocation of the statute presupposed Indian possession of the land in question and that prerequisite for the statute's application was therefore "inextricably entwined with the merits" of the case (see *United States v Wilson*, 433 F. Supp. 57 [N.D. Iowa 1977], at 66).

76. *Omaha Indian Tribe v Wilson*, 575 F.2d 620, 651 (8th Cir. 1978).

77. *Omaha Indian Tribe v Wilson*, 575 F.2d 620, 651 (8th Cir. 1978).

78. Fred Thomas, "Wide Impact Seen in Court's Award of Land to Tribe," *Omaha World-Herald*, April 12, 1978, 2.

79. See "Petitions for a Writ of Certiorari to the United States Court of Appeals for the Eighth Circuit," Supreme Court of the United States, October Term, 1978. See also Fred Thomas, "Attorneys Contend Victory for Indians Threatens Whites," *Omaha World-Herald*, July 28, 1978, 12.

80. Reflecting the national prominence of the case, the attorneys general of thirty other states filed amicus curiae briefs in the Supreme Court, urging the Court to accept the case for review (see "Brief for Amici Curiae in Support of the State of Iowa's Petition for a Writ of Certiorari to the United States Court of Appeals for the Eighth Circuit," Supreme Court of the United States, October Term, 1978, No. 78-161; see also "High Court to Check Indian Land Dispute," *Omaha World-Herald*, November 13, 1978, 1).

81. Douglas Kneeland, "Blackbird Bend a Quiet Battleground," *Omaha World-Herald*, February 19, 1979, 12.

82. *Wilson v Omaha Indian Tribe*, 442 U.S. 653, 99 S. Ct. 2529 (1979).

83. *Omaha Indian Tribe v Wilson*, 614 F.2d 1153 (8th Cir. 1980), *cert. denied* 449 U.S. 825 (1980).

84. See *United States v Wilson*, 523 F. Supp. 874 (N.D. Iowa 1981), in which Judge Bogue held in favor of the Omahas on the issue of title to the state-claimed land; *United States v Wilson*, 707 F.2d 304 (8th Cir. 1982), *cert. denied* 465 U.S. 1025 (1984), in which the Eighth Circuit Court of Appeals once again reversed Judge Bogue, remanded the case for further consideration, and or-

dered the district court to award the Iowa landowners the value of the "improvements" made to the property prior to the Omahas' regaining possession; *United States v Wilson*, 578 F. Supp. 1191 (N.D. Iowa 1984), in which Judge Bogue ruled in favor of the state of Iowa as to the seven hundred acres in dispute and returned the case to Judge McManus for further handling on the issue of "improvements"; *Omaha Indian Tribe v Jackson*, 854 F.2d 1089 (8th Cir. 1988), *cert. denied* 490 U.S. 1090 (1989), in which the Eighth Circuit affirmed the award of the seven hundred acres to the state of Iowa and also affirmed an unpublished decision by Judge McManus awarding the Iowa landowners $1,921,177.85 for the value of the improvements made to the land previously awarded to the Omahas; and, finally, *United States v Wilson*, 926 F.2d 725 (8th Cir. 1991), in which the circuit court held that the government must pay simple rather than compound prejudgment interest on the amount found owing to the Iowans.

85. Wynema Morris, interview with the author, February 5, 1997. See also "Indians Block Surveying of Land," *Omaha World-Herald*, February 11, 1987, 43; and Fred Thomas, "Tribal Arrests Threatened if Disputed Land Entered," *Omaha World-Herald*, March 16, 1987, 32.

86. Doran Morris Sr., interview with the author, February 28, 1997. Morris was chairman of the tribal council from 1981 to 1992 and remains a member of the council today.

87. See "Tribal Leader Calls Judge a Racist," *Sioux City Journal*, June 6, 1987; Kathy Hoeschen Massey, "Monona Land Case Wraps Up," *Sioux City Journal*, June 3, 1987.

88. See Fred Thomas, "Omaha Indian Tribe Sues for More Iowa Land," *Omaha World-Herald*, February 2, 1986, 10-B.

89. Thomas, "Claims Threaten Recreation Tract," 8.

90. William H. Veeder, interview with the author, March 3, 1997.

91. Doran Morris Sr., interview with the author, February 28, 1997.

92. Mary Kay Quinlan, "Indians Lose Financial Backing in Land-Claims Case," *Omaha World-Herald*, March 4, 1982, 12; see also "Tribal Aide: 'Secret Deal' Ends Indians' Legal Fund," *Omaha World-Herald*, March 5, 1982, 3.

93. District Judge Warren Urbom, "Memorandum and Order," May 29, 1990, 10, Case C75-4067, Federal District Court for Northern District of Iowa, Western Division.

94. *Omaha Indian Tribe v Tract I—Blackbird Bend Area*, 933 F.2d 1462, 1471 (8th

Cir. 1991) (per curiam), *cert. denied sub nom. Omaha Indian Tribe v Agricultural & Indus. Inv. Co.*, 502 U.S. 942 (1991).

95. See *Rupp v Omaha Indian Tribe*, 45 F.3d 1241 (8th Cir. 1995). See also Stacy M. Casey, "Tribe Ordered to Pay $417,527," *Sioux City Journal*, April 13, 1993; and "Tribe Considers Judgment," *Sioux City Journal*, April 16, 1993.

96. For contemporary accounts, from the perspectives of both sides, of local reaction to the final decisions in the litigation, see Frank Santiago, "Court Rules against Indians in Blackbird Bend Dispute," *Des Moines Register*, May 31, 1991, in which Veeder described the court's ruling as a "great tragedy" and "another example of how the Indian tribes are being planned out of existence"; Kathy Massey, "Tribe Loses Appeal, Court Rules Land Belongs to Iowa Owners," *Sioux City Journal*, May 31, 1991; Frank Santiago, "Despite Setback, Indians Vow to Fight for Iowa Land," *Des Moines Register*, June 1, 1991; Frank Santiago, "Fickle Missouri Leaves Legacy of Litigation," *Des Moines Register*, June 16, 1991, 1B, 4B, including photographs of key personalities on both sides of the dispute; Kathy Massey, "Tribe Loses Land Battle, High Court Refuses to Hear Appeal, Case among the Oldest in Federal Courts," *Sioux City Journal*, November 8, 1991, 1, A14; and Kathy Massey, "Court Decision Stuns Landowner," *Sioux City Journal*, November 8, 1991, in which one of the Iowa claimants estimates that the group spent more than $200,000 defending their claims and describes himself as "ecstatic" at the news of the final decision.

97. In an unpublished letter dated July 6, 1990, tribal chairman Doran L. Morris asked Senator Joseph R. Biden, chairman of the Senate Judiciary Committee, to investigate "the failure of the Federal Judiciary to fulfill its obligation to provide the Tribe a full and fair trial before a fair tribunal" and to remedy "the forced fraudulent representation [of the tribe] by the attorneys in the Department of Justice." Cosigned and written by William Veeder, the thirty-page letter recited a long litany of grievances against the government attorneys and the federal judges involved in the Blackbird Bend litigation. Although rambling in style and obviously self-serving as to Veeder's culpability in the courts' dismissal of the tribe's claims, it is nevertheless a valuable reflection of the tribe's bitter outrage at the outcome in the Blackbird Bend cases. No formal action was ever taken by the committee in response to the tribe's request. In Veeder's words, "It was simply ignored" (William H. Veeder, interview with the author, March 3, 1997).

98. The notion that the government's trust relationship with Native American tribes is deeply flawed is hardly an innovative suggestion. Just one example of the mass of academic commentary addressing various deficiencies in the trust

relationship is Daniel McNeill, "Trusts: Toward an Effective Indian Remedy for Breach of Trust," *American Indian Law Review* 8, no. 1 (1980): 429–57, in which the author describes the trust as "a vaporous entity, whose shifting, uncertain contours have lent themselves to diverse and contradictory interpretations by different courts" (p. 430).

99. Vincent Willey, interview with the author, February 21, 1997. Other area residents whom I interviewed expressed similar or even stronger sentiments, but all asked not to be identified in print.

100. Wynema Morris, interview with the author, February 5, 1997.

101. One of the internal tribal debates centered on the question of payment of William Veeder's bills for legal services. One faction of the tribe felt that Veeder had "fought the good fight" against overwhelming odds and ought to be paid. Others argued that his actions had cost the tribe its claim for the vast majority of the land at issue and resisted payment. Ultimately, Veeder sued the tribe for payment, and he was finally paid $175,000 in 1993. Tribal member Wynema Morris indicated that the positive view of Veeder's role is the "majority view" within the tribe (interview with the author, February 5, 1997). Doran Morris, council member and former chairman, agreed, stating, "There should be no animosity toward Bill Veeder at all. The land we regained and the benefit we receive from it are a result of his work" (interview with the author, February 28, 1997).

Conclusion

1. For a comprehensive examination of the problems faced by the Omahas in the eighteenth and early nineteenth centuries, see Boughter, *Betraying the Omaha Nation*.

2. A recent and extremely useful exploration of the general mood and status of the reservation is provided in Michael Kelly, "Hope, Problems Combined in Reservation Life," *Omaha World-Herald*, November 24, 1994, 1.

3. Kelly, "Hope, Problems Combined in Reservation Life," 12.

4. Julie Anderson, "Two Tribes Distribute Casino Cash," *Omaha World-Herald*, December 23, 1994, 14.

5. Kelly, "Hope, Problems Combined in Reservation Life," 12.

6. Kelly, "Hope, Problems Combined in Reservation Life," 13.

7. Kelly, "Hope, Problems Combined in Reservation Life," 13.

Index

Aberdeen Area Conference (1957), 27

Abourezk, James, 17

accretion, 91, 105

Adams, Allan M., 10

AIM. *See* American Indian Movement

Alcatraz Island occupation, 89

alcohol, sale of to Indians, 30

Allen, Stephen, 106

allotment, xiv–xv, 18–19; and 1882 legislation, xiv, 16–17; and Dawes Act, xiv; and the Omaha reservation, xiv

American Indian Movement (AIM), 89, 94

Anderson, Harry R., 84

Anderson, Victor, 27, 32

Aoway line, 54, 55 map 2, 56, 140 n.28

Article 2 line, 71

assimilation: of Omahas by allotment, xiv–xv, 1–2. *See also* Indian policy

Association on American Indian Affairs, 31–32

avulsion, 91, 105

Ayoway River (Iowa Creek), 54

Babby, Wyman, 97

Barrett, T. H., 92. *See also* Barrett Survey

Barrett survey, 92, 99, 106–7, 109

Beaver, Gordon, 42

Beck, Clarence S., 14, 27

Becker, Herbert, 97

Bereuter, Doug, 111

BIA. *See* Bureau of Indian Affairs

Black Bird Hills, xiv, 56

Black Bird, xiii

Blackbird Bend I, 109. *See also* Blackbird Bend litigation

Blackbird Bend II, 110. *See also* Blackbird Bend litigation

Blackbird Bend litigation, xvii, 89–113; and 1973 occupation, 94–96; and 1975 occupation, 97–99; burden of proof in, 107; and CasinOmaha, 113; and claims of fraud, 153 n.39, 154 n.46 n.51; and claims of racism, 109; decisions in, 150 n.14; dismissal of claims in, 111; and emotionalism, 91; and movement of Missouri River, 93, 94 map 5; and Omahas' resistance to government representation, 100–101, 153 n.43; and request for Senate hearing, 112, 159 n.97; and riparian rights, 91, 105; Supreme Court ruling in, 108; and trust relationship, 92, 112, 159 n.98

161

Bogue, Judge Andrew W., 105–6, 155 n.62

boycott, 33–34

Bruce, H. E., 11, 12, 14, 21–22, 25

Bruce, Louis R., 42, 93

Bureau of Indian Affairs (BIA), 3, 5, 9, 12; and investigation of Omaha reservation, 39; and jurisdictional issues, 43; presence on Omaha reservation, 25

Burke, Thomas, 108

Butler, Hugh, 5, 7, 8, 14, 121 n.14 n.15, 123 n.31

CasinOmaha, xviii, 113, 114 fig. 4, 115–16

Cession 151, 72, 73 map 3, 75, 80–81

Champe, John L., 57–58, 140 n.33

Chippewas, 75

Civil Rights Act of 1968, 36. *See also* Indian Bill of Rights

Cline, Edward L. (Ed or Eddie), 17, 29, 30, 34, 35, 36, 45, 94–96, 104, 106

Collier, John, xv, 2–4, 6, 9, 120 n.7

Committee on Interior and Insular Affairs, 9, 12, 44, 63, 84

Concurrent Resolution 108, 1, 7

Confederated Sac and Fox tribes (Sac and Fox), 69, 70–72, 75, 79, 144 n.9

Court of Claims, 56–57, 60, 135 n.1

cross-deputization, 43

Curtis, Carl, 93

Davis, W. D., 59, 62

DeLoria, Vine, Jr., 48

Docket 138 litigation, ICC, 69–87; and 1830 treaty, 72–75; appraisals in, 81; childrens' portion of award, 139; and cross-claims, 79; decision on title, 80; and distribution of funds, 86; expert testimony in, 79; final judgment in, 84; Omaha Rule in, 82; and per capita payments, 84; settlement hearing in, 83–84; and severance of Omahas' claims, 82; title phase in, 79–80; and tribal factionalism, 86–87; and tribal investments, 85; valuation phase in, 81

Docket 225 litigation, ICC, 51–67; appraisals in, 59; childrens' portion of award, 66; compromise of, 61; final award in, 60; final judgment in, 62; offsets in, 60; and Omaha Rule, 61–62; and per capita payments, 63–64; title phase in, 57–58; and tribal factionalism, 66–67; and tribal investments, 65–66; valuation phase in, 59; and Winnebago cession, 53

DuBray, Alfred, 86

Dyer, W. Earl, Jr., 29

Eighth Circuit Court of Appeals, U.S., 109, 111

Eisenhower, Dwight, 7, 9, 11

Elliott, John, 26, 30

Ervin, Sam, 35

Executive Order 11435, 39. *See also* retrocession

Fletcher, Alice, xv

Flicker, Anne, 34, 35, 44, 134 n.78

Fontanelle, Logan, 139 n.22, 151 n.16

Fontanelle, Victor, 151 n.16

Freemont, Francis, Jr., 82–83

French, Dale, 30

Friends of the Indian, xiv

Frizzell, Kent, 97, 99, 100

Fuhrman, Mark, 33, 40, 44

Gillan, Ralph H., 16
Gilpin, Alfred, 13, 25, 27, 29, 31, 64, 66, 86, 92
Goham, Wayne, 34
Grant, George, 58

Harrison, William H., 5
Hastings, Dennis, xii
Hickel, Walter, 39, 40
Holt, William M., 78, 81, 137 n.10
Hoover Commission, 4, 121 n.9
House Resolution 5971 (1961), 63
Hruska, Roman, 40, 93
Hultman, Evan L., 100–102, 154 n.51

ICC. See Indian Claims Commission
Indian Bill of Rights, 36, 131 n.44
"Indian Bounty Act," 30. See also Legislative Bill 713
Indian Claims Commission (ICC), xvi–xviii, 47–51; co-opted by terminationists, 48; and interest on awards, 50, 138 n.12; jurisdiction of, 49; and method of valuation, 50; and offsets, 50; and Omaha Rule, 61–62; original goals of, 47; procedures of, 51; and remedial limits, xvii, 50, 135 n.1, 137 n.11; scholarly assessment of, 48, 135 n.4. See also Docket 225 litigation; Docket 138 litigation
Indian Claims Commission Act of 1946, 49
Indian Law Enforcement Improvement Act of 1975, 16
Indian New Deal, xv, 2–4
Indian policy, federal government, xi–xii, 2; assimilation vs. self-determination and, xi, 4, 39; grassroots effects of, xi; and Indian Claims Commission, 47; and trust relationship, 92, 149 n.8; vacillation in, xi, 4, 39, 120 n.2. See also specific subject entries
Indian Removal Act of 1830, 72
Indian Reorganization Act of 1934 (IRA), 2–3, 21
Iowas, 69, 75
IRA. See Indian Reorganization Act of 1934

Jackson, Andrew, 72
Jackson, Harold, 96
Janis, Thomas, 45
Johnson, Lyndon, 39, 85
jurisdiction, transfer to states of, 13; and legislative awareness, 28; Nebraska consent to, 14; Omahas' consent to, 13; and public awareness, 15

Kirk, Joe, 150 n.13
Kitto v. State (1915), 19–20
Klamath reservation, 35
Klamaths, 7, 122 n.27

Lakin, Charles, 150 n.13
Lamson, Amos, 11, 12
Land and Resources Development Association, 86
Large Village, xii–xiii
Lay, Judge Donald, 107
LB 713. See Legislative Bill 713
Legislative Bill 713 (LB 713), 28–29; hearing on, 29, 129 n.20
Legislative Resolution 37 (Nebraska), 38. See also retrocession

Lewis, Orme, 9, 10, 18

Mackay, James, xiii
Madigan, LaVerne, 32
Major Crimes Act, 18, 25, 125 n.55;
    and PL 280, 26, 125 n.57
Mayne, Wiley, 102
McManus, Edward J., 101, 104, 109,
    110, 155 n.59
membership, Omaha tribal qual-
    ifications for, 64, 67
Menominee reservation, 10, 35
Menominees, 7, 122 n.27
Meriam Report, 2, 4
Meyer, Clarence A. H., 16, 38, 40
Miller, Mrs. Howard, 102
Mills, Lawrence C., 69
Missouri River, 92–93, 94 map 5,
    103 map 6
Monona Bend, 103 map 6, 104, 110
Monona County Landowner's Asso-
    ciation, 102, 113
Morris, Doran, Sr., 109
Morris, Wynema, 113
Morrison, Frank, 28
Murphy, Lawrence E., 13
Murray, William G., 59, 81
Myer, Dillon S., 4–6, 10, 11, 121 n.11
    n.13

Nash, Phileo, 65
National Congress of American In-
    dians, 5
National Council of Churches, 154
    n.51
National Farmer's Union, 6
Nebraska, Omaha jurisdiction before
    1953 in, 15–20; BIA investigation
    of, 17; state's culpability in, 19–20
Nebraska Legislative Council, 38

Nebraska Supreme Court, 15–16, 17,
    19
New York Times, 9, 15, 130 n.41
Nixon, Richard, 37, 39, 132 n.55
Northern Ponca. see Poncas

O'Brien, Donald E., 110
O'Brien, John T., 100, 102, 104, 110
Olsen, Arnold, 32
Omaha cession, 54, 55 map 2, 56
Omaha Indian Reservation (Omaha
    reservation), 1, 7, 56; creation of,
    52, 54–56, 92; and failure of PL
    280, 32; and law enforcement,
    20–23; "social problems" on, 21;
    survey of, 92
Omaha Mission Bend, 102, 103 map
    6, 110
Omaha Rule, xvii, 49, 61–62, 82. See
    also Docket 225 litigation; Docket
    138 litigation
Omaha Tribal Council, 12, 30, 34,
    37, 85, 96–97
Omaha Tribe of Nebraska (Omaha
    tribe or Omahas). See specific sub-
    ject entries and individual names
Omaha Tribe v. Village of Walthill
    (1971), 17, 42
Omaha World-Herald, 30, 125 n.54
O'Marr, Louis J., 59, 60, 78
Otoes, 70
Ottawas, 75
Otto, Norman, 28

Pender Times, 33, 125 n.54
Pendleton, Donald, 96
per capita payments, 63, 64; use of,
    64, 65 fig. 1, 83, 116
Peterson, Raymond G., 150 n.13
Pine Ridge reservation (Sioux), 38

Pine Ridge, 89, 101
PL 280. *See* Public Law 280
Platte Purchase, 75, 76 map 4, 81
Poncas, 6, 122 n.26
Portage des Sioux Treaty, xiii
Potawatomis, 75, 80
Prairie des Chiens treaty (1825), 71, 80, 144 n.5
Prairie du Chien treaty (1830), 72–75, 80, 144 n.5
Prucha, Francis Paul, 48
Public Law 280 (PL 280), xvi, 7–15; amendment of, 36; constitutionality of, 13; and disclaimer optional states, 123 n.31; effect on Nebraska jurisdiction, 15–20; Indian consent to, 8, 123 n.38; and law and order on Omaha reservation, 25–27; legislative history of, 8; and mandatory states, 7, 9, 10, 123 n.30; Nebraska consent to, 14; Nebraska legislative awareness of, 28; Omahas' consent to, 10–14; public awareness of, 15, 125 n.54
Public Law 89–717, 85

rape (1969 incident on Omaha reservation), 32–35, 130 n.41
Red Lake reservation, 10
Red Power movement, 89, 148 n.1
Resolution 108. *See* Concurrent Resolution 108
retrocession, xvi, 35–42; attempt to "rescind," 40–42; and highways exception, 43–44, 123 n.70; and Nebraska Legislative Resolution 37, 38; Omaha resolution seeking, 36; "partial" acceptance of, 39–43

Richendifer, Blair, 34
Ridington, Robin, xii
Robinson v. Sigler (1971), 15–18
Robinson, Enoch, 15
Rosebud reservation (Sioux), 38
Rosenthal, Harvey, 48

Sacred Pole (Umon'hon'ti, Venerable Man), xii
Saunsoci, Louis, 66
Scott, T. Harold, 81, 83
self-determination, 39
Senate Bill 1518 (1961), 63
Senate Subcommittee on Constitutional Rights, 35
Seneca, Martin E., Jr., 101
Shell Creek line, 54
Sioux reservations, 30. *See also* Pine Ridge reservation; Rosebud reservation
Smith, G. Hubert, 57–58, 140 n.33
Sorenson, Harold, 108
Springer, Arthur, 86
State v. Goham (1971), 41
Storie, Clyde, 31, 34, 37, 43, 44, 45
Supreme Court, U.S., 108

Tate, Michael, xv
taxation of Indian lands, 28–29, 128 n.17
Ten Haken, Reuben H., 29
termination, 1, 4–8, 13, 121 n.10; and Omahas, 85; repudiation of, 39
Thompson, Morris, 99
Thone, Charles, 93
Thurston County: and jurisdiction over Indians, 27; law enforcement in, 21, 25; statistics regarding, 21, 22 table 1, 23

Trail of Broken Treaties, 89
Treaty of 1854, xiv, 52, 53–56, 75, 92, 94; framed copy at Blackbird Bend, 94, 95 fig. 2
Trottier, Eugene, 43–44
Truman, Harry S, 48
trust relationship, 91–92, 112, 149 n.8, 159 n.96
Tyndall, Dennis, 34
Tyndall, Wayne, 67, 115

Umon'hon'ti. *See* Sacred Pole
Urbom, Judge Warren, 111

Veeder, William H., 111; payment of fees to, 160 n.99
Venerable Man. *See* Sacred Pole

Walker, William F., 39
Wallace, Anthony F. C., 79
Walthill Citizen, 34, 64, 125 n.54
Warm Springs reservation, 10
Washburn, Wilcomb, 48

Watkins, Arthur, 5, 61, 81, 83
Wedel, Mildred Mott, 79
Weissbrodt, I. S., 78
"We Shake Hands," 31
White, Clarence, 66, 86
White, Gustavus, 27, 58
Willey, Vincent, 113
Winnebago Agency, 11, 12
Winnebago Tribe of Nebraska, 40, 41, 44, 53; and Omaha cession, 54–56; and retrocession, 132 n.56
Witt, Edgar, 58, 80
Wolf, Wilson, 82, 83
Wolfe, Clifford, Sr., 108
Wood, Albert, 89, 96, 106, 110
Wounded Knee (1973), 89, 93; juxtaposed with Blackbird Bend, 151 n.19
Wunder, John, 48, 90

Yankton Sioux, 70, 71

Zendejas, Ed, 64, 86, 133 n.70

Other titles in the Law in
the American West series include

Volume 1
Christian G. Fritz
Federal Justice in California
The Court of Ogden Hoffman, 1851–1891

Volume 2
Gordon Morris Bakken
Practicing Law in Frontier California

Volume 3
Shelley Bookspan
A Germ of Goodness
The California State Prison System,
1851–1944

Volume 4
M. Catherine Miller
Flooding the Courtrooms
Law and Water in the Far West

Volume 5
Blue Clark
Lone Wolf v. Hitchcock
Treaty Rights and Indian Law
at the End of the Nineteenth Century

Volume 6
Mark R. Scherer
Imperfect Victories
The Legal Tenacity of the
Omaha Tribe, 1945–1995